MARY DODSON WADE

AMAZING

texas girls

TRUE STORIES
FROM LONE STAR
HISTORY

LONE
STAR
BOOKS

Guilford, Connecticut

LONE STAR BOOKS

An imprint of Globe Pequot

Distributed by NATIONAL BOOK NETWORK

Copyright © 2018 Mary Dodson Wade

Map by Melissa Baker © Rowman & Littlefield

British Library Cataloguing in Publication Information available
Library of Congress Cataloging-in-Publication Data available

ISBN 978-1-4930-3196-2 (paperback)
ISBN 978-1-4930-3197-9 (e-book)

∞™ The paper used in this publication meets the minimum requirements of American National Standard for Information Sciences— Permanence of Paper for Printed Library Materials, ANSI/NISO Z39.48-1992.

Printed in the United States of America

For Jeanne Dodson, sister-in-law extraordinaire;
Jean Everett, West Texas historian, for laughs over "facts"
not being fact; hubby Harold, perpetual proofreader;
Melia and Marisa Wade, two girls in Hawaii
who are pretty amazing themselves.

Contents

Acknowledgments

Researching a project makes authors aware how much they depend on others to help them do their work. This book is no exception. Thanks go to those who helped provide photos—Lisa Struthers at the San Jacinto Museum of History, Houston; Warren Stricker at the Panhandle Plains Historical Museum, Canyon; Margaret Harman at the LBJ Library, Austin; Terre Heydari at the DeGolyer Library, Southern Methodist University, Dallas; Alston Cobourn at the Jeff and Mary Bell Library, Texas A&M University– Corpus Christi, Anne Cook at the Texas Department of Transportation, Austin; and Tomás Pantin, Austin photographer.

Special thanks to Laurel Lamb at the Scurry County Museum, Snyder, who took time to resurrect photos during busy exhibit preparation. A delightful visit with Ingrid Grant at the African American Library at the Gregory School helped identify the photo for Barbara Estrada to release from the Houston Public Library Metropolitan Research Center. Teresa Hedgpeth at the US Olympic Committee in Denver, Colorado, worked cheerfully to "meet specs." Phyllis Earles at Prairie View A&M dug through archives to locate the needed photo. And what a delight to renew contact again with Guadalupe Quintanilla and her assistant Karina Medina!

Introduction

Texas has an amazing history created by some amazing people. This book details the lives of fifteen women who were participants in that story. All but one of them were born before 1920. The period in which they lived ranges from the first permanent Spanish settlement in colonial Texas to the present. Some come from privileged backgrounds, while others struggled with circumstances. In reading their stories, it is often easy to see how their childhood affected their accomplishments as adults. Some of these women are quite well known, some known only locally, and for a few this is the first time their full story has appeared in a book. Nevertheless, these individuals are all part of the incredible story of Texas.

María Gertrudis Pérez Cordero Cassiano

1790-1832

*M*aría Gertrudis Pérez Cordero Cassiano was a woman of independent means. Her family was descended from the Canary Islanders who settled San Antonio, Texas. Her father was wealthy enough to buy the building on the San Antonio plaza that we know today as the Governor's Palace, and she inherited his property when he died. She married a Spanish army general and reviewed the troops for him when he was away fighting Apache Indians. When he died, she married a wealthy Italian. Because Spanish women could own and manage property, she handled her own affairs.

Gertrudis Pérez was born on January 2, 1790, at the Pérez homestead in Villa de San Fernando, the settlement formed with the arrival of Canary Islanders in 1731, forty-five years before the American Revolution. The new settlers named the small community for the heir to the Spanish throne, future king Fernando VI. This first permanent settlement in Texas is known today as San Antonio, one of the ten largest cities in the United States.

A census two years before Gertrudis Pérez was born listed three different components for San Antonio de Béxar—Mission San Antonio de Valero, the presidio of San Antonio de Béxar, and the Canary Islanders' settlement called Villa de San Fernando.

The mission came first. Spain was aware of the importance of having outposts in territory far distant from Mexico City, but it was usually Catholic missionaries who pushed into unsettled territory first in an effort to bring Christian faith to the native inhabitants. For that reason the Spanish viceroy in Mexico City readily approved the request to move a mission from the Rio Grande area to south-central Texas, ordering soldiers to accompany them. On May 1, 1718, Mission San Antonio de Valero, later known as the Alamo, was founded in present-day San Antonio on the east side of the San Antonio River.

Four days later the presidio was in place on the other side of the river, about a musket shot away. Soldiers stationed there were charged with the responsibility of protecting the mission. Some of them brought their families with them, but the little village where these dependents lived did not qualify as a town.

Thirteen years passed before settlers arrived to start a true town at San Antonio de Béxar. That same year, isolated Mission Los Adaes three hundred miles away in East Texas closed and moved to one of the newly established missions along the San Antonio River south of the town. Three other missions, each serving a different indigenous group, opened at the same time. This string of missions, now San Antonio Missions National Historical Park, includes the Alamo, San José, Concepción, San Juan Capistrano, and Espada. All the missions, except for the Alamo, are still active parish churches. In the beginning, the small contingent of soldiers at the San Antonio presidio was responsible for guarding all these missions.

The settlers who came to establish the new town were from the Canary Islands. They were citizens of Spain. Columbus had stopped at the Canary Islands on his initial voyage to the New World. The name for the group of islands comes from the Spanish word *canis* (dogs) due to the large number of them found there.

King Philip V had authorized four hundred families from the Canary Islands to settle in the New World. The order was soon suspended, but fifty-six individuals had already sailed for Mexico, and they continued to San Antonio de Béxar, arriving in 1731.

They were listed as being sixteen families, but one "family" was composed of four young unmarried men. They had permission to organize a town that they called Villa de San Fernando to honor their prince. As incentive to come to this distant place, they were granted property and given the nobility rank of *hidalgo*, allowing them to use the titles Don and Doña.

Gertrudis Pérez' great-grandfather, a tall, slender nineteen-year-old with black hair and eyes named José Antonio Pérez from the island of Tenerife, was one of those in the "family" of young single men. His brother Phelipe, two years older, was part of that group as well.

Some time after arriving in Villa de San Fernando, Gertrudis's great-grandfather José Antonio Pérez married Paula Rodríguez Granado, who was from the island of Lanzarote. She was the young daughter of María Robaína Bethéncourt Granada, known as the widow Granada or Granadillo. Widow Granada had continued the journey to San Antonio de Béxar after her husband's death while the group was still in Mexico. Paula Granada was described as having a fair complexion, round face, flat nose, with black eyes, hair, and eyebrows.

Their son Domingo, Gertrudis's grandfather, became the first Cabo (corporal) in the presidio, and his son Juan Ignacio Pérez was Gertrudis's father. Also a military officer, her father was later known as Colonel Pérez and became interim governor.

The captain of the presidio at the time of the settlers' arrival had laid out the site for Villa de San Fernando with the church at the center. It faced east, and most of the houses were across the plaza from the church, with the rest completing the square. A second plaza on the west side of the church was the military plaza for the presidio.

The cornerstone of the church was laid seven years after the arrival of the Canary Islanders, and the current stone structure was completed in 1755, although significant rebuilding occurred in 1830. Here, Texan James Bowie married Ursula de Veramendi, daughter of one of San

Antonio de Béxar's wealthiest and most influential families.
From the roof of the church, General Antonio López de
Santa Anna flew a red flag to signal "No Quarter" to Alamo
defenders during the Texas Revolution. The church today
is San Fernando Cathedral, still in use, still at the center of
San Antonio.

Three years after Gertrudis was born, Mission San
Antonio de Valero was secularized. No longer used for religious purposes, it became a military site ten years later when
the Second Flying Company of San Carlos de Parras was
stationed there. These one hundred Spanish lancers were
seasoned veterans from the pueblo of San José y Santiago
del Álamo near Parras in southern Coahuila, Mexico. They
were referred to as La Compañía del Álamo or simply El
Álamo. This led to Mission Valero being known as the
Alamo, and its chapel became the iconic symbol of the 1836
battle there during the Texas Revolution against Mexico.

Prior to Texas independence the town's name was
often shortened to Béxar, and there was no reference to
the original three components. A year after the Republic
of Texas assumed control, the city officially became San
Antonio.

About 1804, not long after the Alamo mission was
secularized, Gertrudis Pérez's father paid eight hundred
pesos for the Spanish Governor's Palace across the military
plaza from San Fernando church. The building, once the
home of the captain of the presidio who was also governor
of the province of Texas, has the date 1749 and a coat of

arms above the entrance door. It was laid out in a typical hacienda arrangement with an interior courtyard.

Fourteen-year-old Gertrudis came to live at the governor's palace during the time her father was a lieutenant-colonel of the presidio. It was naturally a place for military and social activity, and Gertrudis became thoroughly accustomed to that life.

As a young Spanish woman, she was carefully sheltered, never leaving home without a *duena* or chaperone, usually an older woman. Much of the life of the community centered on San Fernando church and its feast days. As the daughter of Don and Doña Pérez, she was trained in the elegant social graces of the times. She was educated, probably by the parish priest. Education was considered necessary because a woman could buy and sell property and manage estates should the need arise, such as upon the death of her husband.

Unlike other young girls of that time, Gertrudis did not marry while in her teens. She was twenty-four when Manuel Antonio Cordero y Bustamente petitioned the governor to marry her. Cordero was an educated, cultured gentleman. Born in Cadiz, Spain, in 1753, he joined the Spanish army at age twenty-four. He was sent to America and over his lifetime commanded troops in twenty-five campaigns against Apache Indians. Explorer Zebulon Pike visited him in 1811 and described Cordero as "five feet ten inches in height . . . fair complexion and blue eyes"[1] with his hair slicked back in military style. Cordero had a military bearing and was "well-read and introspective ... one of the ablest Spanish military commanders on the frontier." Marriage to such an important and handsome man would have seemed quite a match for the daughter who was well beyond the age when girls married. The problem was that he was thirty-seven years older than she.

Nevertheless, the marriage took place on January 1, 1814, at San Fernando church with all the pomp and ceremony of weddings for hidalgo families—wedding procession on horseback to the church, flowers, and music, followed by a day or so of dancing and feasting. Andrea Castañón Villaneuva, better known as Madam Candelaria who claimed to have nursed James Bowie at the Alamo, reported that as a young woman she worked for the family as a chocolate maker, providing Cordero's favorite drink morning, noon, and snack time.

Cordero was obviously impressed with his young wife and her capabilities. Because he was often away on military expeditions, he authorized Doña Gertrudis to act in his place. Since she had been reared in a military family, she slipped easily into the role. She was a striking figure as she reviewed troops at the military plaza, riding sidesaddle on a fine horse and wearing a military-style embroidered jacket and flowing skirt. Soldiers called her *La Brigavielle* (Mrs. Brigadier-General).

She was quite capable of the responsibility her husband entrusted to her, but the marriage came to an end after nine years. Cordero had been elevated to the rank of commandant general of the Western Interior Provinces and promoted to field marshal general. In the spring of 1823, during the Mexican Revolution against Spain, he made his way toward Mexico City as a loyal servant of the king. He died in Durango and was buried there. Under Spanish law, Doña Gertrudis's rights as a widow conferred his property to her.

That same year, Gertrudis's father died, and she inherited his property by the terms of his will, although she had an older brother. Doña Gertrudis, now a mature, educated widow of thirty-three, assumed responsibility for the governor's palace. It would remain in the Pérez family for a century. After passing out of their hands, the building fell into disrepair. In 1929 Adina De Zavala, granddaughter of Texas patriot Lorenzo de Zavala, convinced the city of San Antonio to purchase and restore it. The building in the heart of San Antonio is a museum representing life in colonial Texas and is a registered National Historic Landmark. Adina De Zavala was also instrumental in preserving the Alamo.

For three years after the death of her husband, Gertrudis Cordero managed her large estate. Then, on April 12, 1826, she married José Cassiano, a native of San Remo, Italy. He was a year younger than she and a widower when he came to San Antonio after several years as a successful merchant in New Orleans. He bought the original Pérez homestead south of San Fernando cathedral as well as other property and opened a store. Because both of them had property, the couple could easily have been the wealthiest persons in the city.

María Gertrudis Pérez Cordero Cassiano

The Cassianos made their home at the Pérez homestead, and their son José Ignacio Clemente Cassiano was born there on November 18, 1828. Three years later they surely would have been among important guests at the marriage of Texas hero James Bowie to Ursula de Veremendi, who was descended from Canary Islanders as Gertrudis Cassiano was.

Times were troubled during the early 1830s. Settlers from the United States now resided in Texas and pushed back against restraints imposed by the Mexican government. Cassiano was a strong supporter of the Texan cause. He turned his home and store over to the Texans during the Siege of Béxar (San Antonio) in December 1835 when the Texans forced the surrender and evacuation of Alamo troops under command of Colonel Martín Perfecto de Cos, brother-in-law of Mexican President Antonio López de Santa Anna. Two months later General Santa Anna marched into San Antonio and laid siege to the Alamo where the Texans were holed up. Fighting side by side with them were at least eight Tejanos (Texas-born Mexicans). Six weeks after the fall of the Alamo, Texas won its freedom with the defeat of Mexican troops at San Jacinto on April 21, 1836.

But Gertrudis Cassiano was not in San Antonio during this tumultuous time, nor did she act as hostess for important individuals visiting the Cassiano home and ranch. Four years prior to the precipitous events that made Texas an independent nation, forty-two-year-old Doña Gertrudis died of congestive heart failure, the same disease that took her mother's life. She was buried on September 29, 1832, near the altar in one of the chapels of the San Fernando church. Her little son was only four years old. The boy's father lived another thirty years, providing two stepmothers for his young son.

Gertrudis's will had no provision for donations to charity, strange for such a wealthy woman. She was known for generosity during her lifetime and reportedly set aside Saturdays to distribute alms to the poor. The supposition is that she did not wish her wealth to somehow end up in the hands of the Mexican government when church and state were so closely tied. As a woman familiar with government and business dealings, she may have seen this as an option to protect her estate for her son. Her husband did make gifts to both public charities and school funds in her name after her death, explaining that his wife would have desired it.

María Gertrudis Pérez Cordero Cassiano exemplified the wealthy, educated, capable women living in colonial Texas.

INDEPENDENT WOMEN
IN SPANISH TEXAS

María Gertrudis Pérez Cordero Cassiano was only one of the strong, capable women who lived during the Spanish colonial period. Spain and Mexico made more than sixty land grants to women.

One such woman was María Robaína Bethéncourt Granado (1703–1779), who claimed to be a descendant of Jean de Béthencourt, the knight who in 1402 claimed the Canary Islands for his feudal lord Henry II of Castille. Soon after María arrived in Vera Cruz with other Canary Islanders, her husband Juan Rodriguez Granado died. The twenty-eight-year-old mother and her six children continued the journey to the presidio of San Antonio de Béxar to start a new life. She was granted land that included a home on the main square of the town. A few years later, when she married Martín Lorenzo de Armas, her dowry consisted of her home, two large plots of land, cattle, and tools. She had five more children by her second husband but was widowed again in 1769. She managed her business interests the rest of her life. At her death, she owned her home, land holdings with irrigation rights, herds of cattle and horses, a branding iron, as well as personal belongings that included fifteen images of saints, a mattress, a quilt, a woolen skirt, and a chest brought with her from Lanzarote. María Bethéncourt Granado, sometimes known as Maria Rodriguez-Provayna, was Gertrudis Pérez Cordero Cassiano's great-grandmother.

María Ana Cubelo (1713–1785), also born on the island of Lanzarote, was eighteen years old when she accompanied her parents to the New World. The fair-complexioned, gray-eyed girl with chestnut hair charmed Vicente Álvarez Travieso, a native of Tenerife Island. The color of twenty-five-year-old Travieso's eyes and hair matched that of his wife, except his hair was curly. They married before starting to San Antonio de Béxar, where Travieso rose to prominence. He was elected mayor of the Villa de San Fernando and often brought lawsuits to help the new settlers receive equitable treatment for water rights on land around the villa. He made a concerted effort to round up unbranded cattle that had wandered away from mission pastures. This led to cattle rustling charges against ranchers in the San Antonio River valley since the missions claimed all the cattle. When he died in 1779, María Ana inherited Rancho de las Mulas. Her maiden name Curbelo meant "crow," but it was her three hundred head of cattle, second largest herd in the area, that made up much of her wealth. She died in San Antonio de Béxar and her son Tomás Travieso inherited her property.

Well-educated Rosa María Hinojosa de Ballí (1752–1803) was not a Canary Islander. Born to a prominent family in Tamaulipas, Mexico, she married José María Ballí. She helped one of their three sons, secular priest José Nicolás Ballí, purchase the longest barrier island along the coast of Texas. Padre Island is named for him. By terms of her husband's will, she became owner of fifty-five thousand acres of land. The ranch was heavily in debt, but she managed over the next dozen years to clear the debt and greatly increase her land holdings through numerous land deals. La Feria, her ranch headquarters, was in present-day Cameron County A very religious woman, she built a family chapel and endowed churches in Mexico. By the time of her death she owned more than a million acres of land in the lower Rio Grande Valley, some of it in present-day Hidalgo, Cameron, Willacy, Starr, and Kenedy Counties. She had herds of cattle, horses, sheep, and goats, earning her the reputation of first "cattle queen" of Texas.

María del Carmen Calvillo (1765–1856), born in Villa de San Fernando, was the granddaughter of original Canary Island settlers. She was the oldest daughter of Ygnacio Francisco Xavier Calvillo and Antonia de Aroche's six children, three of whom were adopted. After María's father was murdered by his nephew, she gained control of El Rancho de las Cabras (Ranch of the Goats). The ranch in present-day Wilson County had been a source of food for Mission Espada until it was secularized. She defied all the conventions of the day. Before her marriage to Gavino Delgado around 1781, she arranged to keep her maiden name and hold her property separately since it normally would have passed to her husband's control at marriage. She scandalized her neighbors not only by leaving her husband, but also dressing like a man and riding astride a large white stallion. She could shoot and rope as well as any of her crew. Twenty families worked for her. With their help, she handled the fifteen hundred cattle and five hundred goats, sheep, and horses she owned. She built a sugar mill and granary and put in a large irrigation system. Although her neighbors had trouble with raids by native tribes, they left her property alone because she provided them with grain and cattle. The site of Rancho de las Cabras near Floresville is now part of the San Antonio Missions National Historical Park.

Dilue Rose Harris

1825-1914

Dilue Rose had no way of knowing that she would participate in the chaotic times that saw Texas break away from Mexico. She was only eight years old when her father, Dr. Pleasant W. Rose, moved his family from Missouri to the Texas frontier while the area was still under Mexican control. Three years later, her family fled eastward with Anglo settlers to escape advancing Mexican troops determined to crush rebellious Texans. Her highly readable account, begun at the age of seventy-four, is probably the best known source detailing conditions settlers experienced as they slogged through rain-soaked areas in an affair dubbed "The Runaway Scrape."

Near the end of a life lived under four of the six flags that flew over the state, Dilue Rose Harris published her memoirs. A keen observer, she combined her personal memories with a journal kept by her father. His journal was lost, but Dilue Rose Harris left a vivid picture of events that formed an independent Texas.

Dilue was born in St. Louis, Missouri, April 28, 1825. Her mother, Margaret Wells Rose, was a pious, literate woman whose father owned a farm near St. Louis. Dilue remembered Christmas sleigh rides there.

Her father, Dr. Rose, had been an Army surgeon during the War of 1812 and visited burned-out Washington, DC. Health reasons caused him to resign his commission, but when he arrived in Cuba, he was accused of being a spy and spent the next three years in jail there. This experience under Spanish rule, however, did not stop him from moving first to Missouri and then to Texas before either became American territory.

During the time the Rose family lived in Missouri, they knew the family of Stephen F. Austin, the impresario who brought the first Anglo settlers to Texas. Dr. Rose had lived in Virginia for a time, and it's possible he knew the Austins there. Certainly, he knew of Austin's involvement in Texas because of widely published advertisements offering settlers free land.

This Texas enterprise was the grand scheme of hard-driving family patriarch Moses Austin, who wanted to recover family fortunes after business failures in Virginia and Missouri. He planned to accomplish this by bringing Anglo settlers into Spanish Texas, but he died on June 10, 1821, leaving a request that his son Stephen take up the task of restoring family financial security.

The son's sense of duty to his family brought him to Texas immediately. He placed advertisements in the US papers offering free land to settlers. They began to arrive, but the government of Mexico changed so often that

DILUE ROSE HARRIS (1825–1914)

MRS. DILUE HARRIS, COURTESY SAN JACINTO MUSEUM OF HISTORY, HOUSTON, TEXAS

Stephen Austin spent months in Mexico City trying to assure the validity of land titles granted to settlers in his colony.

A dozen years passed before the Rose family arrived on the Texas coast in 1833 after a stormy voyage from New Orleans. It was Dilue's eighth birthday. Her ten-year-old brother Granville and little sister Ella completed the family. The Roses left two small graves in St. Louis—a four-year-old boy and a baby.

To their shock, the new town of Harrisburg had no school, church, preacher, or courthouse, not even a jail. A schooner from New Orleans supplied the two dry goods stores with groceries and other necessities but often missed its twice-a-year appearance.

Dr. Rose bought a horse and medicine and set up practice in the new place, but heavy rain and crop failure, plus a missing supply ship, caused him to move his family about fifteen miles west to the Cartwright farm near Stafford's Point. They made a difficult two-day journey across flooded prairie in late December to their rented home close to the Brazos River. Mrs. Rose described the night they spent on the road surrounded by water and wolves as a "night of horrors . . . owls were singing a funeral dirge, and the wolves and buzzards were waiting to bury us."[2]

As 1834 dawned in their new home, things improved. Mrs. Rose had brought rice, tea, dried apples, and white sugar from New Orleans. Sugar production on the plantation supplied molasses. Cows on the property provided milk. Venison and small game were plentiful, and neighbors shared butchered beef.

Dr. Rose knew little about farming, but his wife's brother, James Wells, had come with them. The brother and sister had grown up working on a farm. Mrs. Rose made butter and cheese. A wheelwright made her a spinning wheel, and it was not long before Dilue was carding and spinning cotton. She also learned to plait horse hair into rope and to weave straw hats for the men to wear in the hot sun.

On trips back to Harrisburg, Dr. Rose purchased his wife's requests. The girls begged for new red shoes. The nice shoes they had worn when they left St. Louis had worn out, and the girls hated the heavy, ugly replacements. Joy over receiving their new red shoes chased all sleep away.

Since the nearest neighbors lived two miles distant, the girls missed having friends. One day their mother sent them to visit neighboring girls. When they returned home, they found a baby sister waiting for them. Dilue wanted to call her Louisiana. Her father preferred the name Texas, but both were outvoted and the baby was named Missouri.

Dilue and Ella played in a "house" they built under four large trees. A log covered with moss provided a place to sit. But in April they lost their playhouse to adults holding court under the grove of trees. William Travis, later Alamo commander, served as lawyer for the defendant accused of branding a neighbor's calf. After the trial, Travis left with the promise to send the girls hair combs to pay for the use of their play place. He also sent them Sunday school books.

Tragedy struck the community when a little boy was run over by his father's cart. Because there was no coffin to bury him, Dilue's mother supplied a large dry goods box. Then, realizing that the family had no nice clothes in which to bury their child, Mrs. Rose gave them the suit belonging to her little boy who had died.

Slavery was technically illegal in Mexican territory, but Stephen Austin allowed plantation owners to keep them. One day, the Rose family saw a large group of Africans approaching. Three men leading the newly arrived slaves had lost the way to their plantation, and all were on the verge of starvation. Dr. Rose allowed them to kill two cows and then alerted the plantation owner to what he had done. The famished men tried to eat the meat raw, but they were held off until it could be cooked.

The Rose family owned no slaves, but occasionally a plantation slave escaped and ran away. Most were caught and punished severely, but one fled west to the Navidad River. Several people saw him, but the Wild Man of the Navidad was never caught. Rumor said he followed the Mexican army south on its retreat after the battle at San Jacinto.

Even though there was no school, Mrs. Rose insisted that the children keep up their studies. At noon they recited for their father or uncle. Occasionally, Dr. Rose hired a teacher during times young people weren't needed to help with planting or harvesting. Dilue and Ella already knew how to read. Older boys like Granville knew arithmetic as well. To help younger students learn arithmetic, Mrs. Rose gave the teacher her cardboard hat box to make math cards so students could drill with them.

Fourth of July celebrations were all day events—women quilted, men talked politics, and young people danced. Fiddle music kept couples on their feet until dawn. Nine-year-old Dilue went to her first dance with no idea how to do the steps. She watched until she figured it out, and then she and her partner danced until morning.

In late 1834, Dr. Rose left with other men to take their baled cotton crop to Brazoria for shipment. Soon afterward, three hundred peaceful Waco Indians arrived on their way to Harrisburg to sell hides. Initially alarmed, the community soon began trading for baskets and beaded moccasins. Dilue watched them as they left. Waco men riding horses went first. Women followed, some with papooses strapped to their backs. They led ponies carrying hides and blankets, pots and pans, and young children in baskets. Dogs trotted along last.

Relations with the Mexican government were often uneasy as colonists chafed under the lack of freedom they had enjoyed in the United States. Skirmishes at the customs port of Anahuac led to several Texans being jailed, and William Travis led a raid to free them. Meanwhile Stephen Austin had been detained in Mexico City by suspicious officials.

Rumors of approaching Mexican forces came and went, but they turned into fact when Mexican troops under

General Martín Perfecto de Cos occupied San Antonio in December 1835. Armed settlers fought back and forced Cos to surrender, causing an infuriated Mexican president Antonio Lopéz de Santa Anna to march into Texas in February 1836.

Anglos and sympathetic Mexicans formed a provisional government and appointed Sam Houston as army commander. Dr. Rose was too old for army service, but Dilue's uncle James Wells prepared to join General Houston. Eleven-year-old Dilue spent the day "melting lead in a pot and dipping it with a spoon to mold bullets" while her mother sewed two shirts and provision bags for her brother.[3]

The family was unsure what to do. As a precaution, Dilue's mother filled a chest with clothes and blankets, and Dr. Rose hid it in the tall cane away from the house. It was well known that the Mexican army was a large force, and that the Texans were not. They needed to be ready to leave at any moment.

When the Alamo fell, panicked settlers fled toward the Sabine River and safety in the United States in such a hurry that uneaten food lay on tables of abandoned houses. The Rose family fled with them with Dilue's brother Granville driving the ox team that pulled a sleigh carrying their belongings and the two younger girls. Dilue and her mother, clutching her new baby, walked until they could ride in a neighbor's cart. Dilue and Ella cried all day after learning that William Travis was dead. They grieved that their mother had not let them bring the little books he had given them.

At the San Jacinto River near Harrisburg, five thousand people were near riot trying to get on the ferry. It took three days for the Rose family to be able to cross the river; then rain-soaked ground bogged the carts causing them to spend the night on the prairie with only cold meat and cornbread to eat before they got to higher ground.

Conditions were even worse at the Trinity River. Measles, whooping cough, and other illnesses were rampant. Dilue's baby sister was gravely ill. It took their group four days to get all the people, carts, and bedding across the Trinity. Others in their party went on eastward, but Dilue's family stopped in Liberty for three weeks. Mrs. Rose was ill and exhausted from nursing the baby and caring for her sick child. Little Missouri died there.

On the afternoon of April 21, 1836, they heard a very short rumble of cannon fire. From his experience with war, Dr. Rose believed the short length of time they heard the sound meant that the Texans had lost. They fled east immediately and traveled most of the night. The next day they heard a man on horseback yelling, "Turn back! The Texas army has whipped the Mexican army. . . . No danger! Turn back!"[4]

As the courier rode on with the news, the Rose family began the journey homeward. As they crossed alligator-infested Trinity Bay, Dilue's sunbonnet blew off. Mrs. Rose begged her husband not to dive in to get it because a man had just lost his life to an alligator there. Without a sunbonnet, Dilue was forced to wear a tablecloth as a sun shade.

At one stop, they found Stephen Austin's sister. At the San Jacinto battleground, Dr. Rose greeted men he had known in Missouri. The family visited the graves of the Texans who had been killed in the battle, but Dilue was glad to leave the gruesome sight of unburied Mexican soldiers.

They passed burned-out Harrisburg, and Stafford plantation lay in ruins. The sugar mill, cotton gin, and gristmill had been destroyed.

It was Sunday, May 1, 1836, when the Rose family arrived home. Their house was wrecked. Floorboards were ripped up, and hogs rooted inside. Dr. Rose's medicine lay scattered amid broken furniture in the yard. Dilue was shocked to see her mother, who never worked on Sunday, begin to wash clothes. And her father, after bringing up the hidden chest, began plowing.

The fortunate discovery of a large cache of corn provided much needed food, and Dr. Rose's cotton bales had survived. He was able to sell them in Brazoria and brought home new bonnets for Dilue and Ella.

While he was gone, Mrs. Rose took in a boarder who opened a school in the shed attached to the blacksmith shop. Thirteen-year-old Granville and friends got a good laugh when two snorting bulls sent the girls scrambling up to the roof before the boys chased the animals away. Dilue and her sister got even by teasing their brother when he and friends went to see the new "city" of Houston advertised by the Allen brothers. All the boys found was a few people camping in a mosquito swamp. The city of Houston did eventually grow, but instead of moving there, Dr. Rose chose land on Bray's Bayou about five miles away.

A grand ball celebrating the first anniversary of the Battle of San Jacinto was announced, but twelve-year-old Dilue was not able to attend because her mother was taking care of a sick neighbor. Boys in the neighborhood got up their own dance, but disappointment struck again. Two pretty Irish girls got all the attention.

By September 1837 the Rose family had a log house on their Bray's Bayou property. They attended church in Houston. At the celebration on the second anniversary of the San Jacinto battle, Dilue's father introduced his girls to President Sam Houston, who kissed them and said, "Dr. Rose, you have two pretty little girls."[5] Dilue was chagrined. She considered herself quite grown.

Two different times Dilue lost the opportunity to dance with the famous unmarried Hero of San Jacinto. Young widows swept her aside each time. She encountered Sam Houston again when her school attended a theater production. Gamblers had grabbed front-row seats and refused to give them up until the president of the Republic of Texas arrived and shamed them into leaving by saying he, the ladies, and children would sit in the back.

Dilue's disappointment over losing the famous dance partner turned to sunshine when she met twenty-two-year-old Ira A. Harris. On February 20, 1839, fourteen-year-old Dilue married the handsome New Yorker. She and Ira lived near Houston until they moved to Columbus, Texas, in 1845. They had nine children before Ira Harris died in 1869. Two of their sons served in the Confederate army and another survived the great 1900 Galveston hurricane.

Dilue often shared her experiences in early Texas and at age seventy-four began to record them. "The Reminiscences of Mrs. Dilue Harris" was published in the Eagle Lake *Headlight* and the *Quarterly of the Texas State Historical Association.*

The woman who gave such a personal picture of the early days of the Republic of Texas died just short of her eighty-ninth birthday at her Eagle Lake home on April 2, 1914.

MOSES AUSTIN

Moses Austin was the epitome of the aggressive entrepreneurs who continually sought to improve their fortunes. His first fortune came when his characteristic energy created a profitable Virginia lead mining and smelting operation that made bullets. He took his bride, Maria (Mary) Brown, to the isolated town of Austinville, and their son Stephen and daughter Emily were born there. Moses's forceful personality made him a community leader, but disaster struck when the company could not fulfill a contract to provide a lead roof for the Virginia state house.

Learning about rich lead deposits in Missouri, Moses Austin uprooted his family in 1798 and crossed into Spanish territory west of the Mississippi River near St. Louis. Austin's confidence, flair, and courtly manners impressed the Spanish governor who granted him permission to purchase land southwest of St. Louis about forty miles inland.

Austin obtained Spanish citizenship, founded the town of Potosi, and threw himself into making the mine profitable. He succeeded to the point that a year later he moved his family into an elegant two and a half story house he called Durham Hall. Four years later, in 1803, the Louisiana Purchase made the Austin family citizens of the United States again.

Because Moses and Maria were from the East Coast, eleven-year-old Stephen was sent to a private school in Connecticut and later attended Transylvania College in Lexington, Kentucky. But a series of misfortunes, mainly a disastrous drop in lead prices, again wiped out Austin finances.

In the fall of 1820 the elder Austin took his Spanish passport and, with his slave Richmond, headed southwest with the intention of obtaining a grant to settle three hundred families in Texas. For his work as administrator he would receive large grants of land that he could sell to recover family wealth.

As a former Spanish citizen, he expected to find eager acceptance of his idea. Instead, the Spanish governor in San Antonio suspected him of being a spy and without hearing his petition ordered him to leave the territory immediately. Rebuffed, more than a thousand miles from home, and with no prospects, Moses Austin left the governor's office and walked into what can only be described as one of the most fateful chance meetings in history. It would literally change the history of Texas.

On the street, Austin was greeted by an earlier acquaintance, a man who called himself Baron de Bastrop. This claim of nobility hid his true identity as a person accused of stealing government funds in his native Holland. In Bastrop's new life, he had become a respected San Antonio official. He took Austin back to the governor, who then sent a favorable recommendation of the plan to the Spanish authorities in Mexico City.

Moses started home jubilant, but the trip turned perilous after their horses and provisions were stolen. Ill and starved, he and Richmond stumbled into American territory near Nachitoches, Louisiana. Two months later he reached home. His petition was granted, but he did not live to fulfill this last dream. His son Stephen Fuller Austin inherited that awesome task.

Cynthia Ann Parker

1826-1871

Cynthia Ann Parker lived in two worlds, one into which she was born and the other an indigenous culture into which she assimilated so thoroughly that she did not wish to return to her Parker relatives. Not once, but twice, she was violently uprooted from the world she knew. The story of her capture in a Comanche raid on the Fort Parker compound at the age of ten is one of Texas's most celebrated tales.

Her return to her relatives twenty-four years later was no less celebrated and no less traumatic an experience than her first forced removal had been. Truth and myth about her return have become so entwined that the task of separating them is difficult. Nevertheless Cynthia Ann Parker was a real person whose story played out on the Texas frontier in the mid-1800s.

Cynthia Ann was born into the large, interrelated family of Parkers. They were typical of families that spilled over the Allegheny Mountains into the continent's midsection, except that the Parkers were more mobile than most. They reached Texas in one generation.

Elder John Parker, a veteran of the American Revolution, and his wife Sarah "Patsey" Dixon Parker had at least thirteen children. The family moved from Virginia after the birth of their oldest son, Daniel, through northeast Georgia, to Tennessee where the youngest son, Silas, was born. Their next move found them in Illinois. All of Elder Parker's offspring were the children of his first wife. After her death, he married Sally "Granny" Duty, the mother of two of his daughters-in-law.

Cynthia Ann Parker was born in Crawford County, Illinois, about 1826. Her father was Silas Parker, and her mother was "Granny" Parker's daughter Lucinda Duty. Cynthia Ann was the couple's oldest child, son John was about three years younger, and Silas Jr. was born shortly before the Parkers left Illinois. Baby Orlena, born at Fort Parker, was three months old when Comanche Indians appeared at their Texas compound.

The family held strict views on religion. Cynthia Ann's grandfather and her uncle Daniel were leaders of an extremely conservative group called Primitive Baptists who differed from other Baptists because they adamantly opposed Sunday schools, Bible societies, missionaries, and theological seminaries.

Advertisements for free land in Texas drew Elder Parker's oldest son Daniel to Texas about 1830. A decade earlier the Mexican government had reversed its policy forbidding American citizens to enter Texas and granted impresario Stephen Austin permission to bring in Anglo settlers.

CYNTHIA ANN PARKER (1826–1871)
COURTESY OF DEGOLYER LIBRARY, SOUTHERN METHODIST UNIVERSITY, DALLAS, TEXAS

At that time only a few towns existed in the state, San Antonio being the largest because it was the center of government. As a plan to ease the burden of protection for settlements, the Mexican government opened up parts of unsettled Texas so that farms and towns could provide a barrier against attacks by various tribes harassing the population.

Daniel Parker planned to move to Texas and establish a church that followed his beliefs. During his meeting with Stephen Austin, however, the impresario explained that Mexican law would not allow Parker to form a church once he got to Texas because individuals entering had to become at least nominal members of the Catholic Church. However, Mexican law did allow established church congregations to come as a group, and they would retain the right to worship in their own way.

Daniel received land and headed back to Illinois where he organized the Pilgrim Predestinarian Regular Baptist Church. The seven initial members increased to eleven before they left Illinois. The number of church members did not reflect the actual count of people making the three-month journey. To become members of a Baptist church, children must have reached the "age of accountability" and make a personal profession of faith. The same profession of faith is required of adults.

In 1833, whole families consisting of individuals of all ages piled into twenty-five ox-drawn wagons and left Illinois for Texas. Daniel Parker and his brother Isaac, settled on land near present day Elkhart in Anderson County, where Reverend Parker continued as head of his church and was active in community affairs until his death.

Daniel Parker's son Benjamin, perhaps named for his uncle Benjamin Parker, was fourteen at the time he entered Texas. Like his father, he had little formal education, but he was a natural leader and easily slipped into the role of community leader. He served many years as pastor of the church his father founded. While a member of the Texas legislature, he supported a proposal for funds to provide for his cousin Cynthia Ann and her daughter after their return from captivity. He and his uncle Isaac Parker would be appointed Cynthia Ann's guardians.

As early as 1830, fiery James W. Parker, one of Elder Parker's middle sons, moved to northwest Arkansas and began making trips to Texas in search of a place to settle. He applied to Stephen Austin for land to settle fifty families, but receiving no reply—probably because of the turmoil between Texas and Mexico—he made application for land in the Austin and Williams grant. In early 1835 he received a league of land—approximately 4,400 acres— north of present-day Groesbeck in Limestone County near the upper reaches of the Navasota River. In addition, James's younger brother Silas Parker, as well as his own son-in-law Luther Plummer received leagues of land. These grants were about sixty miles west of where Daniel and Isaac settled, well beyond most settlements.

For safety, James and Silas built a compound that became known as Fort Parker. The stockade had an outer wall of twelve-foot-high pointed logs sunk three feet into the ground. Blockhouses rose on two corners to provide extra defense positions. Six cabins, their back walls formed by the log stockade, lined the four-acre enclosure. A large gate faced south and a smaller one on the rear granted easy access to the spring for water.

Cynthia Ann's grandfather Elder Parker, his wife "Granny" Parker, and his widowed son Benjamin joined the families of James and Silas at the completed compound in March 1835. Inside also were Samuel and Elizabeth Frost as well as their daughter Malinda and her husband George Dwight. The men had begun clearing land for fields and planting crops. With the fort for protection, cattle, horses, and farms, the families felt they could be safe and self-sufficient in this isolated area.

Elder Parker had experience in negotiating with Indian tribes in other places where he had lived. It was assumed that they could work out a treaty to assure the safety of the compound. None of them were aware that Comanche groups, although they shared the same nomadic culture, did not recognize one head chief. Each band was independent, with its own leaders. A treaty made with one band had no effect on another. This fact would have tragic results for those living inside Fort Parker's walls in the spring of 1836.

Cynthia Ann's uncle James Parker and his wife Martha (Patsy) Duty, another of "Granny" Parker's daughters, had four young children, but their two oldest girls had their own families. Eighteen-year-old Sarah was married to Lorenzo Nixon. Lively seventeen-year-old redheaded Rachel and her husband Luther Plummer already had an eighteen-month-old named James Pratt, and she was expecting their second child when the attack occurred.

Also in the compound was Cynthia Ann's aunt Elizabeth Kellogg, another of "Granny" Parker's daughters.

As spring came in 1836, they were probably unaware of the February events at the Alamo in San Antonio or the April battle at San Jacinto that freed Texas from Mexico. Men of the community worked outside the stockade clearing land and planting crops. Women went about their usual chores of cooking, milking, sewing, and child care. Ten-year-old Cynthia Ann was old enough to take charge of her two little brothers. Some families were building cabins outside the compound walls, but as a precaution nearly everybody returned to the safety of the compound at night.

Early on May 19 several men left to work the fields. James Parker, his oldest son, and both sons-in-law headed out to plant corn in his field about a mile away. Sixteen adults and eighteen children remained in the fort. For some reason the big gate had been left open.

Mid-morning, a party of Comanche, Kiowa, Kitchai, and Wichita Indians rode up. One of them carried a white flag. Those inside were unsure what to do. As Benjamin Parker went out to meet them, Sarah Nixon ran to tell her father what was happening.

Benjamin returned inside and reported that he did not believe the Indians were being truthful in saying they wanted to sign a treaty. Cynthia Ann's father Silas urged everyone to fight, but it was impossible to shut the gate fast enough to keep out attackers. Benjamin, knowing he would probably be killed, deliberately went back out in order to give those inside time to escape. He was immediately surrounded and attacked. Silas raced out to him but was also killed outside the stockade. Samuel Frost and son Robert were killed inside the fort as they tried to escape.

When James Parker heard Susan's urgent alarm, Luther Plummer ran to alert neighbors a half-mile away. Lorenzo Nixon and his father-in-law started toward the fort but met Parker's wife and young children running for their lives. Nixon continued toward the fort while Parker hid his family, then raced back. On the way he met the Dwight family fleeing with Elizabeth Frost and her remaining son.

Elizabeth Kellogg fled with her mother "Granny" Parker and Elder Parker, but they were caught about three-quarters of a mile away. Elder Parker was killed, and "Granny" Parker was stabbed and left to die. Elizabeth Kellogg was pulled on to a horse and spirited away.

Rachel Plummer, afraid that she and toddler James Pratt would not be able to keep up, had waited too long to leave. She was knocked to the ground, then thrown onto one horse while another rider grabbed her son. She witnessed Benjamin's body full of arrows and recognized her grandfather's gray hair among the scalps. After destroying possessions, the Indians killed most of the cattle and stole the horses as they left.

Lorenzo Nixon arrived at the fort just as Silas's wife and four children were being taken. He managed to save Lucinda Parker and her two younger children but watched helplessly as the Comanche rode away with John and Cynthia Ann.

All the captives except one would be returned within a few years. Cynthia Ann Parker had just entered her second world.

Comanche Indians dominated the lower western plains—a vast area called Comancheria. The tribe, originally a hunter/gatherer group of Shoshone descent, obtained horses in the seventeenth century and became the undisputed master of the territory where they roamed. Their wealth was in horses that furnished them the mobility to hunt buffalo grazing by the millions on the flat, open country east of the Rockies.

Following the attack on Fort Parker, the raiders rode with their prisoners until midnight, celebrated, then continued north for five days, well beyond the reach of any rescue attempts. Each captive was taken by a different band of Indians and later traded to others. Elizabeth Kellogg, taken by Kichai Indians, was ransomed a year and a half later from some Delaware Indians. She had been abused, but not to the extent her niece Rachel endured during her two years of captivity, an ordeal she documented.

As months went by, Rachel was taken farther and farther from Fort Parker, into the mountains of Colorado and beyond. They moved constantly, rarely staying in one place more than two or three days. On the plains the men hunted buffalo, leaving to Comanche women the hard work of curing meat, preparing hides for clothing and tents, and setting up and breaking down camp.

Rachel became the slave of two women, one of them an older woman. Slow at the unfamiliar work assigned to her, she was beaten by her owners. She was raped. When her second child was born that October, she named him Luther for his father, but at six weeks he was pulled from her arms, apparently for taking too much of her time. She watched as the men dragged him through cactus, then flung his torn, lifeless body at her. She dug his grave. She had no tears left to cry.

Rachel assumed that her little boy James Pratt was dead as well. She never saw him after the first few days. She grieved for him till her death, never learning that he survived.

Only near the end of her captivity did Rachel fight back when her younger owner began to beat her. Expecting to be killed on the spot, she turned and beat her tormentor almost senseless. To her surprise the crowd simply watched. Rachel took her younger owner into the tent and treated the wounds.

The men enjoyed the spectacle, but the furious older woman tried to burn Rachel alive. Rachel fought back with such fury that the tent pole was broken in the struggle. The council ruled that she had to repair the damage. Now able to speak enough of the language, she defended herself saying that she did not start the fight and that the other two should be made to help her. The men agreed. After that Rachel received better treatment that she felt came from their respecting her display of courage.

Not until her return did she know of the efforts of her father to find her and the others. James Parker's fury, his obsession with finding the Fort Parker captives, drove him like a mad man. He appealed to Sam Houston, president of the newly formed Republic of Texas, for a force to punish the captors. Houston advised him to negotiate, but Houston did pay the $150 ransom for Elizabeth Kellogg because Parker had run out of money.

James Parker continued his efforts, making seemingly impossible treks into Comanche territory. He offered rewards and raced to identify returned captives only to be disappointed not to find his daughter Rachel. After two years, he felt sure he had located her and arranged with Mexican traders to ransom and deliver her to Santa Fe, New Mexico. Political turmoil there caused her guardians to race with her to Independence, Missouri, where her brother-in-law Lorenzo Nixon met her and brought her back to her husband in 1838. But she died a year later, still grieving for her little boy who had been captured with her.

After seven years of searching, James Parker found both his grandson and Cynthia Ann's brother John. Parker recognized his grandson from the resemblance to Rachel. The boy was still quite young, and he was able to readjust to society, but teenage John escaped and returned to Comanche life. Conflicting stories relate what happened to John, but the most prominent one takes him on a raid into Mexico where he became ill and married the woman who nursed him back to health, never returning to Texas.

Parker's frenzied near decade-long efforts, however, failed to find Cynthia Ann. She was still fourteen years away from returning. And it would not come through James Parker's efforts.

When ten-year-old Cynthia Ann entered the Comanche world, she was adopted by a couple, and she became Naudah. She forgot her own language and became part of this new culture. She learned skills required of women. She married Peta Nocona, and they had two sons, Quanah and Pecos, as well as a little girl named Topsannah (Prairie Flower).

Naudah's life was that of work required of a Comanche woman. For that reason on a cold day shortly before Christmas in 1860, she was among a band of fifteen women, children, and a few Mexican male slaves preparing meat and hides for winter. They were breaking camp just south of the Pease River in present-day Foard County in North Texas near the Oklahoma border when a force composed of Texas Rangers and US soldiers swooped down on them.

In the twenty-four years since her family's disaster at Fort Parker, settlers had kept moving west. As Indians struck back against this invasion of their hunting grounds, the US government built a north/south line of forts across Texas to keep the two groups separated. Soldiers were ordered to punish Indians who raided settlements, and Texas Rangers had the same goal.

On December 19, 1860, twenty Texas Rangers under Lawrence Sullivan (Sul) Ross and a few soldiers from Camp Cooper, an isolated North Texas outpost, charged the hunting camp, shooting indiscriminately. The unarmed Comanche, clad in buffalo robes against the cold, fled, leaving behind forty horses and a winter's supply of meat. According to a diary kept by one of the soldiers, a search of the battle site revealed the bodies of three men and four women. A few Comanche escaped but three were captured. One was a Mexican boy pushed off while riding double. He would be taken home by Sul Ross and given the name Pease Ross.

Naudah, carrying little Topsannah beneath the folds of her buffalo robe, fled on a gray horse but was overtaken. No one there spoke Comanche and she spoke no English or Spanish. Grieving deeply, she kept repeating "Nocona." Charles Goodnight, a scout for the Rangers, spoke with her and understood this to mean she was a member of the Noconi band. Others thought she was saying Peta Nocona's name. That led to the belief that one of those killed was her husband. The myths had begun.

Sul Ross reshaped the story later as he ran for governor, claiming he had killed the great chief Peta Nocona and that the escapees included Quanah. This was refuted by Quanah himself, denying that his father was a chief or that either of them was at Pease River that day.

The myth swelled with each retelling, and the Comanche multiplied into several hundred "warriors." The glory of being part of the recapture of Cynthia Ann Parker inspired "eyewitness" accounts by men who were not even there. The real tragedy lay in the fact that Naudah's blue eyes revealed she was not Comanche. Cynthia Ann was again wrenched from the life she knew.

She was taken to Fort Belknap. Knowledge this could be his niece brought Isaac Parker to see if this could be his brother Silas's child. Cynthia Ann gave no sign of recognition or understanding what the interpreter was asking. The interpreter suggested to Parker that captives would most likely respond to their name. Parker stated that if this were the right person, her name was Cynthia Ann. She repeated her name, pointing to herself.

Instant notoriety followed. Schoolchildren paraded past her in Fort Worth. A photographer tried to take a picture of her, but she bolted, frightened by the equipment. She was brought back, and the photograph shows the face of the thirty-four-year-old woman staring back, revealing her blue eyes and years of living outdoors. The look is that of caution, not knowing her fate, and of sadness. Her hair is cut short, a sign of Comanche mourning.

Isaac Parker took his niece to his home where he now lived about ten miles northeast of Fort Worth. The Parkers sought to welcome her back to the family, but she tried to escape, wanting only to return to the Comanche. She felt restricted in the tight clothes. Sometimes she would build a fire in the yard and stare through the smoke at the sun. She and Topsannah preferred to sleep on the buffalo robe on the floor. Cynthia Ann loved Topsannah fiercely—the only remaining link to her husband and sons.

Isaac's daughter-in-law Mattie Parker had a son Topsannah's age, and she tried to model for Cynthia Ann what to do. She was the only person Cynthia Ann responded to.

Isaac Parker, seeking funds for her support, took her to a meeting of the Texas Legislature. She again bolted, perhaps thinking this was a great council assembled for her trial. Through the persistence of Isaac Parker and his nephew Daniel, she was awarded one hundred dollars for five years as well as a league of land, but her son Quanah was never able to locate and claim it.

In the spring of 1862, Cynthia Ann's brother Silas Jr. came and took her to his home one hundred twenty miles east in Van Zandt County, separating her from her only friend Mattie. When Silas joined the Confederate army, Cynthia Ann moved nearby to the home of her sister Orlena and husband J. R. O'Quinn. Her expert ability to tan hides and braid ropes provided some income.

Bright, lively Topsannah adapted well. She learned to read and write English, but sometime before she was eight, Topsannah died of an illness that could have been diphtheria or smallpox or something called "brain fever." The loss of her child severed Cynthia Ann's last tie to the Comanche world and left her inconsolable.

Some reports said that Cynthia Ann died of a broken heart soon after. The date is not known, but the 1870 census lists Cynthia Ann, age forty-five, as living with Orlena's family, and the most reliable report fixes her death as March 1871. Her notoriety was long over, and no newspaper carried an obituary. She was buried beside Topsannah, still not knowing the fate of her sons. To her death, she grieved for them as deeply as Rachel Plummer had for her son.

Cynthia Ann never knew that one of them would become the celebrated Comanche leader Quanah, the one Parker who would bridge two worlds.

After Peta Nocona and Quanah's brother Pecos died, Quanah, now a Quahadi Comanche, became a leading warrior. Other Indian tribes were forced onto reservations in Indian Territory. The Quahadi under Quanah's leadership resisted. For years they roamed the Panhandle, chasing the ever diminishing buffalo and raiding as they pleased.

All efforts to force them onto the reservation failed until 1874 when soldiers from the 4th Cavalry under the command of Ranald Mackenzie surprised Quanah's group wintering in Palo Duro Canyon. Their life depended on their horses. After routing the Comanche and taking fourteen hundred horses, the soldiers slaughtered all but three hundred of them. At last Quanah was forced to lead his band to the reservation in southwestern Oklahoma.

He refused to be defeated, however. Quanah simply adapted. He learned to speak English. The government appointed him chief of all the Comanche bands, and the tribe accepted his leadership. He became a strong advocate for them. He counseled them to "walk the white man's road."[6] He took his own advice and became a successful farmer and rancher. He was a major stockholder in a railroad. He educated his children. He made appearances before Congress to represent his people's interest.

But he remained a Comanche, adapting some of the "white man's road" for his own purposes. In Cache, Oklahoma, he built a huge two-story home with wide verandas for his seven wives and their children. He played host to a great variety of guests, but he painted twelve stars on the roof of his big house so that he could outrank any general who happened to visit.

Rather than joining a Christian denomination, Quanah organized the Native American Church and argued before the legislature for the use of the hallucinogen peyote in its ceremonies. He is reported to have said, "The White Man goes into his church house and talks *about* Jesus, but the Indian goes into his tipi and talks *to* Jesus."[7]

His friend Charles Goodnight arranged buffalo hunts for Quanah on Goodnight's JA Ranch, the location of Palo Duro Canyon. Quanah attended the 1904 World's Fair in St. Louis and the following year rode in Theodore

Roosevelt's inauguration parade. He went on hunts with
Roosevelt, who was instrumental in having buffalo placed
on the Comanche reservation.

Quanah added Parker to his name and longed to find
his mother's grave. He wanted to bring her to Oklahoma
so that he could lie in a grave beside her. A year before
Quanah died, his son-in-law located Cynthia Ann's grave
and brought her back as well as the remains of a small child
assumed to be Topsannah. The two were buried together in
Post Oak Mission Cemetery near Quanah's home. In 1911,
he was buried beside them . . . in full Comanche regalia.

But they would not stay there. In 1957 the Army
wanted the area for a missile range. With the approval
of the Comanche, all three were reburied with honors in
the Fort Sill Post Cemetery. A tall granite monument in
the section called Chief's Knoll marks the graves of the
woman who lived in two separate worlds and the son who
lived in both.

THE PARKER FAMILY IN TEXAS

This list includes the Parker family members mentioned in this story and members of the Frost and Dwight families.

Elder John Parker, killed at Fort Parker, Cynthia Ann's grandfather
married first to Sarah White – had at least thirteen children
married second to Sallie "Granny" Duty Elder Parker's children:
Daniel, [Eldest son] established Baptist church, settled in Anderson County
Benjamin, [son of Daniel Parker] lived in Anderson County, appointed Cynthia Ann's guardian
Isaac, [Second son later lived near Fort Worth, legislator, appointed Cynthia Ann's guardian
Benjamin, [Third son] killed at Fort Parker, both wives had died before he came to Texas
James W., [Fourth son] married to Martha, daughter of "Granny" Duty Parker
Rachel, [daughter of James and Martha] captured, married to Luther Plummer, mother of eighteen-month-old James Pratt Plummer, [James and Martha's grandson] captured
Sarah, [daughter of James and Martha] married to Lorenzo Nixon
Silas, [Fifth son] killed at Fort Parker, married to Lucinda, daughter of "Granny" Duty Parker

Cynthia Ann, [daughter of Silas and Lucinda] captured

John, [son of Silas and Lucinda] captured

Silas Jr., [son of Silas and Lucinda]

Orlena, [baby daughter of Silas and Lucinda]

Elizabeth Duty Kellogg, [Probably widowed, daughter of "Granny" Parker/sister of Lucinda Duty Parker, lived with her parents Elder John and "Granny" Parker] captured,

Samuel Frost, [Relation to Parkers unclear, perhaps church members] killed at Fort Parker, married to Elizabeth

Robert, [son of Samuel and Elizabeth Frost] killed at Fort Parker

Malinda, [daughter of Samuel and Elizabeth Frost], married to George Dwight

Mary Ann "Molly" Dyer Goodnight

1839–1926

Mary Ann Dyer Goodnight never had any children of her own, but she mothered five younger brothers after their parents died. She served as nurse, teacher, sister, confidante, and comforter to the men working on her husband's ranch. And she could be called "Mother of the Buffalo" for preserving this American icon when she rescued two orphaned buffalo calves.

Mary Ann Dyer was born September 12, 1839, in Madison County, Tennessee. Although the man she married always called her Mary, to everyone else she was Molly. She was the oldest child and only daughter of Joel Henry and Susan Lynch Miller Dyer. Her father was a prominent Tennessee lawyer, her mother the great-granddaughter of Tennessee's first governor. Both parents were educated, and Molly received a fine education at their hands although she never attended a formal school.

For reasons not clear, Dyer left his position in Tennessee and moved his family to Fort Belknap in Young County, Texas, in 1854. Nine years before they arrived,

Texas had dissolved its status as a republic and joined the United States. Although families in the eastern part of the state lived in relative peace, frontier areas were the scene of clashes between incoming settlers and Indian tribes, particularly the Comanche as they lost hunting grounds.

To protect the settlers, the US government built a line of forts stretching across the state from Fort Worth on the north to Fort Duncan (near Eagle Pass) on the Rio Grande. This effort to keep the two groups separate, however, quickly became obsolete as settlers pushed past them.

The government then built a second line stretching in a zigzag from the Red River to the Rio Grande. These forts, built shortly before the Civil War, became the training ground for both Union and Confederate officers who served during that conflict. Robert E. Lee, Confederate commander, had been at Camp Cooper and was called to Washington and offered command of the Union army. Instead, he resigned his US Army commission and became commander of the southern forces. Although Texas itself was far away from major battles, many officers who commanded troops in them had seen service at Texas forts.

Fort Belknap, built in 1851 near present day Newcastle, Texas, was the northern anchor of this second line of forts. Its location on a fork of the Brazos River about seventy miles south of the Red River made it especially important. Fourteen-year-old Molly and her family arrived three years after it was established.

MARY ANN "MOLLY" DYER GOODNIGHT (1839–1926)

PANHANDLE PLAINS HISTORICAL MUSEUM, CANYON, TEXAS

That same year the government set up the Brazos Indian Reservation twelve miles south of Fort Belknap. The peaceful Caddo, Waco, and Tonkawa tribes were moved to the eastern half of the reservation and one branch of Comanche Indians to the western part. Poor land and cultural habits hampered efforts to teach the tribes to farm. Food became scarce, and raids on local farms outraged settlers. They were further alarmed when the Army provided weapons to Indians serving as scouts. Racist newspapers fanned settler anger to the point where they blamed Indians for anything that occurred. After several violent incidents the government closed the Brazos reservation and sent its occupants to Indian Territory (Oklahoma), where hostile Indians slaughtered most of the peaceful Indians a few years later.

By the time Molly was twenty-four, both parents were dead. With the two oldest boys gone, Molly taught school to support her younger brothers Leigh, Sam, and Walter. One story says she met Charles Goodnight while riding with a military escort to a new job in Weatherford, Texas. It's possible she met him through her older brothers who were in the cattle business. Goodnight, three years her senior, already had a reputation for stamina and unflinching courage through his work as a Texas Ranger. He was among the group that brought Cynthia Ann Parker back from her years among the Comanche.

By 1864 Goodnight had left the Ranger force and returned to Black Springs Ranch, which he had established for himself and his mother. His ranch was about halfway between Fort Belknap and Weatherford, where Molly held a teaching position. They met only occasionally as Goodnight drove himself relentlessly to become established as a rancher. When he was free, he came to Weatherford to see her.

Goodnight's opportunity for success came with the longhorn cattle roaming in unsettled parts of West and South Texas. Thousands of wild cattle, hardy descendants of Spanish cattle, were free for the taking. They survived on less water and were disease resistant. Men began to round them up for shipment north. In Texas one steer might sell for six dollars, but cities in the north and east would pay ten times that much.

To profit from the longhorns, the cattlemen had to get them to market. The solution was to round up cattle and drive them long distances to a railhead where they could be shipped to market. Charles Goodnight's name became synonymous with cattle drives.

Partnering with fifty-four-year-old Oliver Loving, an experienced trail driver, Goodnight made his first trip with cattle at the age of thirty. Instead of heading straight north as other drovers were doing, the partners headed their long-horns west into New Mexico, marking Goodnight-Loving trails into Colorado and Montana.

On June 6, 1866, they headed two thousand steers out of Fort Belknap on their first drive. They followed the Butterfield Stage route in a southwesterly direction to Horsehead Crossing on the Pecos River in West Texas before turning north into New Mexico. Horsehead, one of few places to ford the Pecos River, earned its name from the bones of animals that died in the quicksand or from drinking its alkali-laced water. Goodnight called the treacherous Pecos the "Graveyard of the Cowman's Hopes."

Although nature and the Indians took a large portion of their first drive, Goodnight and Loving made a profit by selling beef to Fort Sumner. Goodnight headed home with the gold to gather another herd.

Tragedy struck the second drive when Oliver Loving and "One Arm" Bill Wilson encountered Indians. In action replayed in Larry McMurtry's *Lonesome Dove*, severely wounded Loving fought off Indians for two days while Wilson walked nearly two hundred miles to intersect the Goodnight herd. Loving crawled to a trail where traders discovered him and carried him to Fort Sumner.

Learning that his partner was still alive, Goodnight saddled a soft-gaited mule and made an epic nonstop 110-mile ride to reach him. Two weeks later Loving died of gangrene as a result of his injuries, and Goodnight made good on his promise to take Loving's body home to Weatherford six hundred miles east. He then spent two years of intense work driving cattle to settle their accounts and make sure the Loving family was secure. Meanwhile, Molly continued to teach school and Goodnight visited her during the times he came back to Texas.

Just east of the Rockies, he found an area with grass and water to establish a home base. Here, near Pueblo,

Colorado, he fattened herds before sending them north. He planted orchards and dug irrigation channels to improve hay production.

With finances secure, he headed to Hickman, Kentucky, to marry Molly at her uncle's house on July 26, 1870. Molly insisted that her three youngest brothers make the long trip back to Colorado with them, and Goodnight put the boys to work on the ranch.

The night the Goodnights arrived in Pueblo, two thieves were hanged from a telephone pole, the immediate punishment for cattle rustling. Molly, the daughter of a judge, was so horrified at this disregard of the law that she demanded to be taken back to Texas. Her husband, however, persuaded her to rest a few days and then arranged for her to meet some of the women of the town. Molly settled into life as the wife of a respected citizen. Goodnight owned property in town, pledged money to build a school, and helped establish a bank. Molly led the drive to build a Methodist church. Then, the panic of 1873 wiped out everything.

Molly went to stay with relatives in California while her husband returned to Texas to start again. Exploring the Texas Panhandle, he found Palo Duro Canyon, recently used by Comanche and Kiowa Indians. This great gash in the flat, treeless southern end of the Great Plains had sheer walls rising a thousand feet or more. The canyon floor, twenty-five miles wide in places, followed the Prairie Dog Town fork of the Red River. It offered abundant grass, with cedar and mesquite trees fed by water from springs—the perfect location for a ranch.

Molly, impatient to join her husband, telegraphed that since he was not coming out to civilization, she was coming to him. He was instructed to meet her in Denver in two weeks. He raced to get there, and the Texas Panhandle became Molly's home for the rest of her life.

With money supplied by British entrepreneur John Adair, Goodnight began to build the JA Ranch, using Adair's initials for its name. On the four-hundred-mile trip from Colorado, Molly drove a wagon while Goodnight, Adair, and Adair's socialite wife Cornelia rode horseback the entire way. Goodnight was used to living in the saddle, and the Adairs were excellent equestrians.

Adair's arrogant ways soon riled everyone. Even the usually calm Molly was annoyed at breakfast one morning. Adair objected when a cowboy took his place at the table, stating that he and Lady Adair did not eat with servants. Molly informed him that anybody good enough to work on the ranch was good enough to eat at her table. The Adairs moved. To the credit of New York aristocrat Cornelia Adair, cowboys did eat at her table after her husband's death.

The Adairs' visit was mercifully short, and Molly was left the sole white woman in the Panhandle of Texas. The nearest town was two hundred miles away. Several months later, she was delighted to hear that Mollie Bugbee and her husband Thomas had become their neighbors . . . seventy-five miles distant.

Mary Ann "Molly" Dyer Goodnight

Molly often rode with her husband as he labored to build a successful ranch. He devised a two-horned side-saddle for her comfort. As surrogate mother for Leigh, Sam, and Walter, Molly understood the men working on the ranch, and they idolized her. She studied local plants and concocted home remedies for different ailments. She baked cakes and sent food to the riders working far from the home ranch. She patched clothes and darned socks, taught ranch hands to read and write, and on Sundays held church. In a show of appreciation, the cowboys ordered a silver tea service for her from New York.

Molly's sacrifice was not lost on her husband. Several years later he bought a tall clock and inscribed it:

> In Honor of Mrs. Mary Dyer Goodnight, Pioneer of the Texas Panhandle. For many months in 1877-78, she saw few men and no women. . . . She met isolation and hardships with a cheerful heart and danger with undaunted courage. With unfailing optimism, she took life's varied gifts and made her home a house of joy."[8]

But the most treasured gift for her came the day a cowboy rode up with three chickens. They did not go into the cook pot. Instead, she made pets of them. "No one can ever know what a pleasure those chickens were to me, and how much company they were. They would come when I called and they would follow me wherever I went, and I could talk to them."[9]

Her mothering extended to buffalo calves. These animals, actually American bison, once roamed the plains by untold millions. But by the late 1800s they faced extinction from hunters seeking hides. Small, orphaned calves were left to starve beside the rotting bodies of their mothers. Molly Goodnight persuaded her husband in 1878 to rope two calves and provide a place to keep them. These became the foundation of the Southern Plains buffalo herd, genetically distinct from those on the north plains.

Buffalo from the Goodnight herd would be shipped to Yellowstone National Park and the New York zoo. Others were given to Indian tribes to start their own herd. More than a century after Molly persuaded her husband to rope those two buffalo calves, the JA turned the herd over to Texas Parks and Wildlife. Their home now is Caprock Canyons State Park, just a few miles from where the herd originated in Palo Duro Canyon.

For eleven years, Goodnight labored to make the JA profitable, looking after Cornelia Adair's interest after John Adair died. Finally, right after Christmas 1887, Molly and Charles Goodnight left Palo Duro Canyon and moved about thirty miles north to a stop on the Fort Worth and Denver railroad. They built a substantial two-story house that was their home for the next forty years. Pens held their herd of 250 buffalos, and Goodnight experimented with "cattalo" by breeding cattle with buffalos.

The town of Goodnight eventually grew around them, and they took an active part in developing it. Molly, a staunch Methodist, enlisted her husband in building a church. They took care of relatives and paid for their education. Molly's great love of teaching led them to build Goodnight College where students worked to pay tuition. The college held a significant place in the Panhandle until a state school opened in 1910 in Canyon, Texas.

Young college students filled their house; some even lived there while attending school. One resident, the orphaned sister of the housekeeper, attended college and became Goodnight's secretary. The rancher, whose formal education ended when he was nine, was a serious student of the land and everything connected with it. He spoke forcefully and eloquently, but his handwriting was so bad that sometimes not even he could read it.

Cleo Hubbard, the son of another housekeeper, became the Goodnight's foster son. He was ranch manager and inherited Goodnight's saddle and half of the ranch when it was sold.

Although Charles Goodnight could be gruff, Molly endeared herself to all who knew her. She died April 11, 1926, at age eighty-six. Her husband of fifty-six years sat through only part of Molly's funeral before returning to their house to sit alone in the parlor they had shared so long. Three years later he was buried in the cemetery at Goodnight, Texas, next to the woman who earned the name "Mother of the Panhandle."

CATTLE DRIVES

Cattle drives have become a romantic symbol of the Old West, but they were actually grueling work. Typical cattle drives had several thousand steers, usually belonging to several different owners. Cattle carried the owner's brand and a trail brand as well to identify that particular drive. This helped to separate herds when stampedes sent one herd careening into another nearby on the trail.

Ten or so cowboys kept the herd moving. A trail boss scouted the route, a pointer led the way, swing riders along the side kept cattle from scattering, and those on drag at the back pushed along the laggards. Riders in the rear ate dust kicked up by the herd. A leisurely pace of ten to twelve miles a day allowed the cattle to graze and not lose weight.

Cowboys ate whatever food the cook prepared. Perhaps the cook was a crippled cowboy with no cooking skills, but he ruled the chuck wagon, the unique invention of Charles Goodnight. For his first trail drive Goodnight modified a regular wagon by building a mini pantry at the back end. The back panel swung down to form a table propped up by a post, leaving shelves open to give the cook access to flour, salt, canned goods, and cooking utensils stored there.

Bedrolls were thrown onto the wagon each morning, or they got left behind. The cook did not pick them up. Bedrolls consisted of a tarp with everything the cowboy owned rolled inside—money, a sougan or quilt made of wool scraps, extra shirts, and perhaps letters.

Choking dust, stampedes, dangerous river crossings, cattle crazed for water, and the possibility of encounters with Indians or cattle thieves made the trip dangerous. Cowboys slept on the ground, worked in all kinds of weather, endured monotonous food, and went without sleep to make sure the cattle reached the railroad where they would be shipped to market. Only then did they get paid for their hard work.

Prior to Civil War small cattle drives had delivered beef to St. Louis and New Orleans, but in the 1860s the great cattle drives north began. They lasted until the end of the 1880s when barbed wire, patented by Joseph Glidden in 1874, fenced pastures and cut off routes. In that short time, America produced its greatest folk hero, the cowboy.

ELIZABETH ELLEN "LIZZIE" JOHNSON WILLIAMS
(1843–1924)

Elizabeth Ellen "Lizzie" Johnson Williams

1843–1924

Elizabeth Ellen Johnson was a prim and proper teacher. How then did she become a flamboyant cattle queen, an author of magazine stories under a name nobody ever knew, and a wearer of silk and taffeta dresses with huge diamond accessories? The story of the woman who made the first cattle drive up the Chisholm Trail with her own herd might be a cautionary tale. Sometimes, getting to the top can leave you with no friends. This is the story of a woman who knew what she wanted, and she took it.

Lizzie, the name by which she was known almost all her life, was born in Cole County, Missouri, on May 9, 1843. Her father Thomas Jefferson Johnson was a teacher, as was her mother Catherine Hyde Johnson. Their second child Lizzie grew up with three brothers and two sisters in a family steeped in education.

Thomas Johnson taught for four years in Jefferson City, Missouri, before moving his family to Texas when Lizzie was four. Texas at that time had just become part of the United States. Most of the population was in the eastern part of the state, and the Johnson family first went to Huntsville where Senator Sam Houston, former Texas president, had his home. After a short time, Johnson moved to positions in Lockhart and then Webberville about fifteen miles east of Austin.

Professor Johnson was very religious and felt a call to establish an institute that would provide both good educational opportunities in this sparsely settled area and one that would also bring it religion. He felt that educated, moral citizens would ensure a stable community with good government. He was particularly opposed to liquor because it caused people to act in ways that were inconsistent with religious and moral values.

In 1852 he chose Bear Creek in Hays County as the place to build Johnson Institute. According to a family story, the city of Austin offered land for Professor Johnson to build his school there. Austin, near the western edge of populated areas, had served as capital of the Republic of Texas and remained the state capital when Texas entered the Union. In the early 1850s its population was fewer than a thousand residents. Politics was the dominant business, and a school of higher learning would enhance the community. Johnson turned them down. He was convinced the "city" had too many evils, that saloons would be detrimental to his students. The University of Texas main campus occupies that land today.

The Johnson Institute was located instead about seventeen miles southwest of Austin. Originally planned to provide education for boys only, the institution opened as coeducational after many girls asked to attend. The fact that Johnson's daughters could not attend an all-male school may have entered into the decision as well. Lizzie and her siblings were educated there, and several of them, including Lizzie, later taught at the school.

The first buildings were log cabins that the students helped to construct. These would be replaced later by a substantial two-story, ten-room limestone building. In addition to providing space for classrooms, it housed boarders. At its height, the school had several hundred students enrolled, including both boarders and day students.

To provide for students' spiritual needs, headmaster Johnson invited ministers from various congregations to speak at assemblies. Attendance for Sunday services was mandatory for the students, and neighboring ranchers and farmers were welcome to attend as well. If no preacher was available, Johnson himself gave a lecture on some Bible story. In warm weather, services were held outside under the live oaks.

The school curriculum stressed grammar and spelling, but students studied a variety of subjects. Professor Johnson taught higher mathematics. After receiving a degree in 1859 from Chappell Hill Female College near Brenham, Lizzie returned to the Institute to teach French, arithmetic, bookkeeping, and music. The Institute's piano was the first one in Hays County. Lizzie's nephew remembered her as a strict disciplinarian like her father, whose ideas about religion and liquor she adopted.

Unfortunately, Professor Johnson died in 1868, the year the new building opened. His wife and children kept the Institute running for a few more years, but it closed permanently in 1872. After having several owners, the building now belongs to a religious group and has been so significantly modified that it no longer has historical marker identification.

By the time Johnson Institute closed, Lizzie was teaching elsewhere. She went first to Lockhart, then Manor, and to Oak Grove Academy in Austin before she opened her own primary school in the state capital. She bought an Austin lot and lived in the four upstairs rooms while teaching classes on the lower floor. She continued to run the school until 1880, but she was already earning money from other sources.

Some of her money came from writing stories for one of the publications of the Frank Leslie empire. Leslie produced several magazines that appealed to different kinds of readers. *Frank Leslie's Illustrated Newspaper*, later renamed *Leslie's Weekly*, had been founded the year after Johnson Institute was established. It covered news stories and patriotic events for the next seventy years. The magazine for women featured fashions and fancy needlework. *Boys' and Girls' Weekly* provided stories for children. All were illustrated with very good photos or artwork—Norman Rockwell created some of the later covers for the magazine. Leslie's name was so well known that, following his death, his suffragette wife changed her name to Frank Leslie to carry on his enterprise.

Elizabeth Ellen "Lizzie" Johnson Williams

There is no way to know what Lizzie Johnson contributed. She wrote under a pseudonym, perhaps to conceal her identity or because it was assumed men would not read anything written by a woman. Nevertheless, women did write. New England author Louisa May Alcott, famous for her children's books, was a contributor to *Frank Leslie's Illustrated Newspaper*. Alcott's romances, however, were written anonymously.

All the time Lizzie wrote for the magazine, she kept teaching, carefully saving the proceeds. When she finally accumulated twenty-five hundred dollars, she invested in a Chicago cattle company. She turned this initial investment into twenty thousand dollars at the end of three years. With this money, she began to buy land and cattle.

Bookkeeping provided Lizzie's third source of income. The state capital naturally drew cattlemen, and she began to keep business records for some of them. She knew prominent cattlemen like George Littlefield and William Day. With her insider's knowledge of the cattle business and the amount of money to be made, she made a decision to go into the cattle business herself.

On June 1, 1871, she bought a herd of cattle along with its brand, then went to the Travis County courthouse and recorded the CY brand under her name—Elizabeth Johnson. But she had other plans for her money.

Two days after registering her brand, she dipped into her savings and bought ten acres of land in Austin, paying for it with three thousand gold dollars. This was the first of her very secretive land ownership transactions. Once, when her brother wanted to buy some land in Austin, he discovered that his sister owned the property.

At thirty-six years of age, Lizzie Johnson was wealthy and unmarried when she met a charming widower named Hezekiah Williams. They married on June 8, 1879. Hezekiah had several children by his first wife, but Lizzie never had much interaction with them.

Although he was a preacher, Hezekiah had a bad problem with alcohol. In spite of her feelings about liquor, Lizzie loved Hezekiah. But she had managed her own finances too well too long to mix her earnings with his. At that time, when a couple married, a wife's money came under the control of her husband. Lizzie would have none of that. Before they married, Hezekiah had to sign an agreement that whatever she owned before their marriage stayed under her control and any future earnings from it would remain her separate property as well.

It's not clear if he knew how much money she had, but he should have gotten a clue from the wedding dress she chose. Their wedding photograph shows tall, bearded, dignified Hezekiah standing beside a rather somber bride wearing a gorgeous dress of the latest fashion. Tucks and bows decorated the front of the skirt, a bustle draped down the back, and lace decorated the neck and cuffs. Lizzie was six inches shorter than Hezekiah, but her extremely tall flowered hat reached higher than his head.

Elizabeth Ellen "Lizzie" Johnson Williams

For a while after marriage she continued to teach at their Austin home. Hezekiah got into the cattle business with his own brand two years after marriage, and they bought a ranch near Driftwood in Hays County, the only property that they owned jointly.

They went together to stock sales, and Lizzie stood by the chute choosing the cattle she wanted. She told the stock handler to put the good ones in her herd because Hezekiah would probably lose his anyway. Their herds were never mixed, but Lizzie did the bookkeeping, carefully recording expenses and the hours each cowboy worked.

Although their herds were separate, they used the same foreman to manage both. According to a family story, Lizzie told the foreman to put her brand on all of Hezekiah's unmarked calves. But Hezekiah had given the foreman directions to put his mark on all her unbranded calves. The foreman carried out both sets of instructions.

Lizzie's decision to retain management of her own money was a wise one. She was correct about Hezekiah's business ability. She often bought and sold quickly, but Hezekiah waited, expecting to get a better price but losing money in the deal. In some cases she kept him from bad decisions, but in others she just bailed him out when his business enterprises failed. At one point, she had to cover a fifty-thousand-dollar debt for him. Then, when his finances improved, he had to pay her back.

This was the period of the great cattle drives. There was money to be made by delivering cattle to railheads where they could supply beef to cities in the North. The price for a steer there was ten times the price paid in Texas. Lizzie did not intend to miss this opportunity.

Usually, herds from several owners were thrown together until the number reached at least two thousand animals. Only Richard King of the immense King Ranch in South Texas and Abel "Shanghai" Pierce, who ran a large cattle company, had herds large enough to trail north with only their own livestock.

The Williamses sent their herds in mixed drives. A cowboy who picked up Williams's cattle in 1885 and 1886 remembered multiple stampedes with the first herd. He described it as having "run" on the mind the whole way. The cattle looked so bad on arrival they waited before delivering them so the animals could gain back some weight. The misfortunes that occurred on that drive fit Hezekiah's luck.

Twice Lizzie and Hezekiah themselves took the Chisholm Trail with cattle carrying her brand. The cowboys liked her and respected her knowledge of cattle and her business skills. Alert and observant, she spoke their language and had a remarkable memory for names. She took note of her cattle daily.

The days were hot. Dust rose from the moving mass. Cowboys worked in all kinds of weather, sleeping on the ground and eating whatever the cook offered. But Lizzie did not share all of the hardships on the trail. She and Hezekiah traveled in a buggy. Dressed in calico and wearing a bonnet and gray shawl, her only worry was to deliver her cattle safely. She did that and earned the title of cattle queen. Once the cattle were delivered and the cowboys headed home, she and Hezekiah went to St. Louis where she bought expensive things.

Besides their cattle business, the Williams tried to create Hays City on their property, hoping to move the county seat there after the courthouse burned in San Marcos in 1908. They built a church, but only two streets were ever finished—one named Johnson, the other Williams. The county seat remained where it was.

Lizzie kept buying real estate. In downtown Austin, she owned the Brueggerhoff building at East Tenth and Congress Streets and lots on East Sixth Street and West Twenty-Sixth. She had land in Llano and Trinity Counties as well as small ranches in Culberson and Jeff Davis County.

The couple began to spend a lot of time in St. Louis. They stayed in the best hotels, and Lizzie bought fashionable velvet and taffeta dresses trimmed in braid and lace. On a trip to New York, she spent ten thousand dollars for a pair of earrings made with two-carat diamonds and a tiara with a three-carat diamond center surrounded by nine half-carat diamonds.

For several years they lived in Cuba, selling cattle. Some reports said Hezekiah was kidnapped and that she paid fifty thousand dollars for his release. It is true that Lizzie brought back a talking parrot that she kept for years. On their return, a banker met the ship in Galveston with flowers for her and escorted them to a hotel room filled with flowers. Lizzie was not impressed. She often said she preferred cowboys because they would do anything for her, but bankers only wanted her money. She was more likely to hide money in her room than put it in the bank.

Hezekiah's problem with alcohol ruined his health. During the last twenty-five years of his life, they sought cures at places like the mineral baths at Hot Springs, Arkansas. Then, in 1914 they went to El Paso hoping a different climate would improve his condition, but he died while they were there.

For all of her crustiness, the seventy-one-year-old widow loved Hezekiah and did not hesitate to buy him a six-hundred-dollar casket. She brought his body back to Austin and across the funeral bill, in language that might have shocked her father but not the cowboys who knew her, scrawled "I loved this old buzzard this much."[10]

Now alone, she did not care what she looked like. Her behavior became erratic. Occasionally she appeared in public with her jewels. She attended a movie in the 1920s wearing all her finery . . . in a dress forty years out of style. On the Austin streets, she could be heard hailing legendary cattle-man George Littlefield, "Hey, you old cattle thief!"[11] The dignified bank owner simply bowed in reply. As time went on, she was seen on the street wearing a long black skirt and her forty-year-old gray shawl. She looked so shabby that people gave her money because they felt sorry for her.

She moved to the upper floor of the Brueggerhoff building, cramming her things into a small apartment and storing the rest in the basement. She was miserly with building tenants, allowing them only one stick of firewood at a time. Once, her niece came when Lizzie was sick. She placed several sticks of firewood in the stove to warm the damp apartment, then went down to get more from the well-stocked firewood room. When she came back, one stick was again in the stove and several charred pieces on the wood stack.

Lizzie had an agreement with the owner of the restaurant on the first floor for one ten-cent cup of vegetable soup each day. When he tried to go up to fifteen cents, she refused to pay, citing their contract. In the last years of her life, the restaurant sent up meals that she thought were free but had been paid for by her relatives.

Churches and schools including the University of Texas made appeals for donations. She never refused outright, instead keeping them hopeful. But she had no intention of parting with her money.

By 1923 Lizzie became unable to live alone. Her niece took Lizzie into her own home. The doctor ordered eggnog for the undernourished woman. Because Prohibition was in force, he had to write a prescription for the alcohol. Lizzie, the teetotaler, thoroughly enjoyed her "nutritional supplement." She was pleased with the comforts there, but her mind became more confused. She slept during the day and roamed the house at night mumbling, "This is the wrong street, the wrong street!"[12]

Lizzie Johnson Williams died October 9, 1924, at the age of eighty-one. She left no will. When that happens, the state places a value on the person's assets and determines the heirs. Travis County Probate Court listed Lizzie's estate at $188,441.12 (about three million dollars in today's money), but there was probably an error because after debts were settled, the remainder was almost that amount.

Her bank account had about fifty-three thousand dollars, but nobody knew where to look for the diamonds. They had last been seen in 1916 when Lizzie nearly upstaged the bride at her nephew's wedding. A search of the Brueggerhoff apartment yielded hundreds of five-dollar bills hidden behind a boarded-up bookcase panel and hundred-dollar bills stuck in crevices. Altogether it amounted to twenty-eight hundred dollars. But the diamonds were nowhere in sight.

The search extended to the Brueggerhoff basement. Locked boxes were pried open, but they contained only parrot feathers and flowers from Hezekiah's funeral wreath. Then, in a little unlocked box, a folded piece of scorched cloth opened up to reveal the diamond jewelry.

Lizzie never cared for Hezekiah's children and had little to do with her own family except the favorite niece with whom she spent her last year. Hezekiah's children received approximately $18,500, and Lizzie's nineteen nieces and nephews shared equal amounts of the remainder when Lizzie Williams's holdings were sold.

Elizabeth Johnson Williams is buried beside Hezekiah in Oakwood Cemetery in Austin, Texas. The woman who lived life on her own terms—admired by some, disliked by others—was a distinct individual, eccentric and domineering. She was not afraid to speak her mind nor fearful to engage in a world dominated by men. But wealth hoarded does not foster friendship or ensure happiness. Lizzie Johnson Williams may not have cared.

Amanda Burks, who also accompanied her husband on a cattle drive, drove her little buggy from Corpus Christi, Texas, to Newton, Kansas, while her husband worked the cattle. But she traveled with a helper who put up her tent every night and took the reins when she was tired. She experienced lightning storms, encountered Indians, had confrontations with farmers, and enjoyed summer fruit on the three-month journey. A cowboy observing her remarked that he would have felt sorry for her except "when I see your smile of happiness and contentment I know all my sympathy is wasted."[13]

Amanda Burks agreed. "For what woman, youthful and full of spirit and love of living, needs sympathy because of availing herself of the opportunity of being with her husband while at his chosen work in the great out-of-door world?"

Lizzie Williams, cattle queen, would probably have changed the focus of that to being able "to do exactly what she wanted to do." Because of doing what she wanted to do, she was inducted into the National Cowgirl Hall of Fame and Museum in 2013, nearly a century after her death.

THE CHISHOLM TRAIL

One of the best-known cattle trails was the Chisholm Trail, named for Jesse Chisholm. He was born in Tennessee to a Cherokee mother and a father of Scottish descent. After his parents separated, Jesse went with his mother to eastern Oklahoma when the Cherokee were removed from Tennessee.

He learned five languages and served as a scout and an interpreter, but his name is better known for the cattle trail. He owned trading posts at the north and south borders of Indian Territory and marked a path between them to facilitate moving goods. When Texans began driving herds north, they used his trail across Indian Territory.

Texans extended his name to the Texas part of the route as well. Herds from various places in South and Central Texas met near San Antonio and headed almost straight north to the railroad in Abilene, Kansas.

An estimated five million head of cattle were "pointed north" on the Chisholm Trail before it closed in 1884 due to quarantine and fencing. The ban against Texas cattle went into effect when it was discovered that farm cattle died after longhorns passed through the area. Longhorns were immune to the disease that was carried by ticks clinging to their hides. Cattleman "Shanghai" Pierce correctly identified ticks as the carriers of the fatal "Texas Fever."

The westward movement in the United States was aided by rail lines reaching farther west. Cattle trails were forced to move west as well. The Western Trail went to Dodge City, Kansas. The Goodnight-Loving route ran through New Mexico and Colorado to Wyoming.

Christia V. Daniels Adair

1893–1989

C hristia Daniels Adair was a fighter, not with fists but with actions, working through political organizations, clubs, and church groups to gain dignity, education, and civil rights for African Americans. She forced people to confront prejudice and injustice by her insistence on being treated as an individual, not as a member of some subculture. She broke down barriers for people of color—opening Houston's public library, airport, government offices, and department store facilities. At the dedication of the Houston city park named for her, the chairman of the Harris County Democrats commented, "She was a bridge between the races. . . . She had a gracious manner that enabled her to say things which other black people could not say without stirrup up hostility."[14] At her memorial service, Harris County commissioner El Franco Lee stated, "She helped to make this city, state, and nation a better place for people of color. With poise, grace and quite a bit of steely strength . . . she moved our dreams ahead."[15] For civil rights accomplishments, Christia Adair took her place in 1984 among former first ladies, astronauts, and Olympic athletes in the Texas Women's Hall of Fame.

Christia V. Daniels was born in Victoria, Texas, on October 22, 1893. Siblings included older stepsister Althia and two younger brothers, Webster and Gus Reed. Her father, Hardy Daniels, had a hauling business. He and Christia's mother, Ada Crosby Daniels, set high standards for their children.

Christia's grandfather died when she was about two, and the family moved to Edna, twenty-five miles east of Victoria, to take over the grandfather's business. The company hauled cotton and personal belongings for families. It employed several workers who wore jumper-like gingham shirts made by Ada Daniels. She washed and ironed the shirts so that every employee had a clean one to wear each day. The men ate breakfast and lunch with the family, instilling in the Adair children that everyone should be treated equally.

Each evening the family gathered at the dinner table about eight o'clock. After prayer, Hardy Daniels explained something he had heard or knew that involved politicians and law enforcement. The children had to sit and listen even when they were bored. Christia credited those sessions with helping her gain an understanding of politics that served her well later in life.

Strong religious faith guided family actions. One source lists Hardy and Ada Daniels as being among six families who founded Scruggs Chapel Methodist Episcopal Church in Edna, but conflicting information says the church was founded about a dozen years before her family moved there.

CHRISTIA DANIELS ADAIR (1893–1989)

Regardless, her parents were leaders in the Edna church
and the children took part in its activities.

Scruggs Chapel was affiliated with the African Methodist Episcopal Church, founded in 1817 by former
slave Richard Allen. The Methodist movement, begun by
Englishman John Wesley in America, broke away from
the Episcopal Church following the Revolutionary War.
From the beginning, the denomination focused on service,
calling for active personal involvement with those who
were sick, poor, dying, or exploited. Membership included
the wealthy and also poor laborers and even slaves. Working in the church and being guided by the goals of social
work learned there prompted Christia's actions the rest of
her life.

When she entered first grade in 1900, segregation was
in full force. The only school open to African-American
children in Edna was substandard, overcrowded, and ill
equipped. Fifty desks were available for over a hundred
children. Teachers at the white schools were paid ten times
more than the principal and two assistants at the school
for African Americans. Christia attended the Edna school
through sixth grade.

A family friend, John W. Frazier, was concerned over
the level of education the Daniels children were receiving. He had met Christia's father while teaching school in
Victoria, and through that friendship became Christia's
godfather. Frazier had studied both at Bennett Seminary
in Greensboro, North Carolina, and Wiley University in

Marshall, Texas. He and his wife moved to Austin, Texas, in 1900, and he partnered with Reuben S. Lovinggood to found Samuel Huston College.

This private school for African-American students was established through the Freedman Aid Society and supported by the Methodist Church. It was named for Samuel Huston of Marengo, Iowa, and merged with Tillotson College some fifty years later. The historically black school, now known as Huston-Tillotson University, has approximately one thousand students on its east Austin campus and is still affiliated with the United Methodist Church.

One interesting side note about the influence of Samuel Huston College some thirty years after Christia Adair attended the school involved legendary baseball player Jackie Robinson. He accepted the offer to be the school's athletic director as a result of his friendship with the college president. Robinson coached the 1944-45 baseball team and when he didn't have enough players, put himself in the lineup for exhibition games. His teams had little success, but he was respected as a coach. Two years later, when the Brooklyn Dodgers signed him, he became the first African American to play in the major leagues. His number 42 is the only one that has been retired across teams in all leagues. Robinson was respected for his character, his stand for nonviolence, and his tremendous baseball talent. In 1984 President Ronald Reagan posthumously awarded him the Presidential Medal of Freedom, the highest civilian honor an American citizen can receive.

At the time Christia entered Samuel Huston, black "colleges" had both elementary and secondary students due to the poor foundation students received at segregated public schools. They also offered college-level courses and some even had graduate courses. High schools had two tracks—one for vocational work, the other college preparatory. Samuel Huston's high school followed the vocational track. Curriculum there was the same as public school, except two hours of Bible study a week were required as well as daily chapel attendance to which the student had to bring both a song book and their Bible.

Professor Frazier, the school librarian, taught mathematics. He convinced Hardy Daniels to send Christia to Samuel Huston to get a better education. Although never wealthy and not educated themselves, Christia's parents valued education. They paid tuition not only for Christia but also Webster, a year and a half younger, to keep the two together. The Fraziers acted as surrogate parents and modeled dignity and service for Christia.

Entering seventh grade at fifteen, Christia graduated elementary school the following year when the school had an enrollment of 262 elementary students, ninety-five secondary, and twenty-six college students, with a faculty of nineteen. She stayed two more years to complete her high school requirements at the age of eighteen.

In the meantime, during the summer between elementary and high school, Christia was called to the bedside of the terminally ill Sunday school superintendent in Edna.

The woman told Christia she wanted her to become the new superintendent. When Christia protested, the woman replied that she could learn. Ada Daniels asked her daughter how she responded, and she said. "I couldn't do anything but say yes. She's a dying woman."[16] Her mother reminded her that she couldn't break her promise. At sixteen, Christia was Sunday school superintendent at Scruggs Chapel Methodist Church. Her religion professor that fall helped her fulfill her promise.

After she graduated from Samuel Huston, Hardy Daniels encouraged his daughter to take teacher training at Prairie View Normal and Industrial College. Teaching was a highly respected vocation for African-American women, and the pay was much better than other employment. But it also meant more years of study. At that time it was possible to take an examination to enter at an advanced level and graduate in two years. Christia passed the examination and entered as a junior, receiving certification to teach domestic science and graduating in May 1915 at the age of twenty-one.

She returned to Edna and taught in the elementary school for two years at a salary of thirty-five dollars a month. When she was asked to teach in the county school, her father advised her to ask for a raise. The county school in Vanderbilt paid her forty dollars a month. She learned to speak for what she wanted.

Her teaching career ended when she married Elbert H. Adair in 1918. Elbert worked as a brakeman for the

Missouri Pacific Railroad. He made good wages and did not want his wife to work.

They moved to Kingsville, and that is where Christia began her long career of volunteer service and social work. She and her husband joined the Methodist church. Attendance was low, and the first thing she did was organize a Sunday school. She knew that if the children came, the parents would too. Church attendance increased as she expected.

An incident involving one of her Sunday school students triggered her involvement in community activism. She observed the high school boy coming out of a gambling house rather than being at school. "And it just put war-fire in me . . . and I found out he wasn't the only teenager that they were using at the tables, to make money."[17] Realizing she needed the help of all mothers, not just African Americans, she took African-American mothers to visit the woman who was president of the all-white Mothers Club. Because the gambling facility was a menace to all the youth in the community, the woman advised Christia to organize a Mothers Club to get people involved.

The two groups worked together, and the sheriff heard about it. Since he was profiting from the gambling house, he subpoenaed Christia's group to appear in his office to explain their actions. Elbert was concerned. He was sure the sheriff's "court" was illegal, but Elbert's schedule meant that he had to leave town before Christia was scheduled to meet with the law officer. He advised his wife to appear as

instructed but not to tell the sheriff anything. The women
followed that advice, and the sheriff decided that it was all
talk. The mothers, however, contacted the district attorney,
who called a real court. Christia could not have been more
pleased with the result. "And it ended up with this sheriff
having to go and nail up the building himself and we were
on the sidelines rejoicing and praising God."[18]

One of Christia's major goals was to be able to vote.
Working through the political system, she diligently col-
lected signatures on petitions asking that women be allowed
to vote. When Texas granted women the right to vote in
the primaries, she arrived at the polling place early with
a group of African-American women, only to have the
election official turn them away. They refused to leave until
he finally confessed that African-American women were
not allowed to vote. This only served to intensify Christia's
efforts. When the Nineteenth Amendment granted all
women the right to vote, Texas became the first state in the
South to ratify it.

The Republican Party had many African-American
members because of its close association with Lincoln and
the end of slavery. Christia was proud to be a Republican,
and she looked forward to voting in the 1920 election for
Republican candidate Warren G. Harding.

As part of his campaign, Harding rode on a train that
stopped in various towns to let him greet voters. Because
of Elbert Adair's seniority, he was usually on the train
that brought officials to Texas. While aboard candidate

Harding's train, he noticed schoolchildren at each stop shaking hands with the candidate. He called Christia to tell her. She raced to the school to alert the teachers to bring their students to the Kingsville train station to see the man who might become the next president of the United States. Since the teachers could not dismiss school, Christia got permission from parents and arrived at the station with about a dozen children. She often met Elbert's train and knew about where the last car would stop. She stationed her children so they would be closest to the candidate when he got out to talk with people. Her children were right by the steps, but Harding completely ignored them and reached over their heads to shake hands with the white children. Angry, disappointed, and hurt for her students, she pulled them out. It was a decisive moment for her. "If that's what Republicans do, I cannot be a Republican. . . . From here on out I'll have to work for Democrat presidents."[19]

In 1925, after Elbert developed diabetes and could no longer work a heavy schedule with so little time to rest, the Adairs moved to Houston. He worked an easier shift on the passenger train between Houston and Brownville.

The couple immediately joined Trinity Methodist Church, the oldest black church in Houston, then two years later moved their membership to the Boynton United Methodist Church where they remained members until their deaths. Christia became chairperson of the Christian Social Concern program, carrying out Methodist goals of ministering to the disadvantaged. That service would lead to her being the first African-American woman to serve on the national board of the Christian Social Relations Department, a position she held for eight years. When she was eighty-four, Trinity Methodist celebrated her life and accomplishments, also celebrating her inclusion in the 1977 Black Women Oral History Project conducted by the Schlesinger Library at Radcliffe College.

As a new Houston resident in the mid-1920s, Christia plunged into other activities involving women. She joined the 1906 Art, Literary and Charity Club, the oldest African-American federated women's club in Houston. Both white and African-American women had formed clubs of this type as a way to study and become aware of political issues even before they could vote. At regularly scheduled meetings, members presented papers they had prepared on subjects of interest to the women, keeping them informed about people and issues. The clubs funded scholarships, established kindergartens, and provided leadership training for women.

The Art, Literary and Charity Club was affiliated with the National Association of Colored Women's Clubs. Christia began six decades of active membership in this organization that worked to educate African-American women who had experienced little opportunity to advance. There was a general perception that uneducated African-American women lacked morals and therefore could not possess culture. The organization focused on providing guidance and example so that disadvantaged women could rise above their current situation. With the motto of "Lifting as we climb,"[20] the women worked through their clubs and churches to combat stereotypes and racism and gain quality education for their children.

Christia was involved with Girls Clubs where adults taught manners, etiquette, and how to dress to young women. The girls were trained in public speaking and escorted to state competitions. They were encouraged to get an education and to keep striving to achieve. Christia's influence was such that one of the Houston chapters was named for her.

She joined the National Association for the Advancement of Colored People (NAACP), where, next to her church, she felt she fit best. After Elbert died in 1943, she came into leadership roles. She spent three years as administrative assistant to the executive secretary of the Houston chapter before assuming leadership for the turbulent years 1950–1959. She was responsible for recruiting members, handling correspondence, and was on the forefront, collecting sworn statements and photographs to document discrimination and harassment of African Americans. Because the local organization lacked money, she was never paid.

NAACP activities resulted in extreme efforts to shut down the Houston branch. At one point representatives of the Texas attorney general entered their offices and turned the place inside out looking for evidence to use in a trial in which the NAACP was accused of soliciting cases that could lead to school desegregation lawsuits. They particularly wanted membership rolls. Knowing that NAACP membership would get an employee fired, Christia spent five hours on the stand but revealed nothing. The trial went on for fifteen days, and it was never established whether there were membership rolls or not.

As a model for her "steely" response, Christia recalled an incident in which Edna officials asked her father to use his influence in the African-American community to support an action that he recognized would not benefit all of his people. He refused and officials threatened to stop using his hauling business. Hardy Daniels became furious, telling them they were asking him to sacrifice his principles and give wrong advice to his friends.

During her four decades as a community leader in Houston, Christia Adair helped open libraries, universities, and public schools to African Americans. When school desegregation became final, she personally went door to door to let mothers know that their children could attend the school nearest to them.

In department stores, clerks sent African Americans to the alteration room at the back of the store rather than allowing them to use the fitting rooms to try on clothes. Christia, who was quite thin, asked to try on a girdle. When the clerk directed her to the alteration room, she insisted she didn't need alterations and that the fitting room would be fine. The clerk called the manager, who allowed her to use the fitting room. Christia paid twenty-nine dollars for a girdle she didn't need in order to make her request legitimate. This action opened department store dressing rooms to African Americans.

She consistently tried to work interracially. One of her big allies was Houston mayor Roy Hofheinz, who served from 1952 to 1956. The mayor, better known as the developer of the Astrodome, which he called the Eighth Wonder of the World, was the son of a laundry truck driver. Perhaps this heritage made him sympathetic to the causes Christia espoused. His help proved invaluable.

At Houston's only airport in the mid-1950s, African Americans could sit only within a square of four benches. They could not buy food nor use any restrooms except for one facility for both men and women down a very long dark hall. When the city upgraded the terminal at Hobby Airport, they refused federal funds to circumvent desegregation of the facility. When it opened Christia called Mayor Hofheinz to tell him that the Whites Only signs were up at the new facility. He forced their removal.

The only library open to African Americans was woefully equipped. When Hofheinz learned of it, he called the NAACP and told Christia to urge everyone to get a library card because the public libraries were open to everyone.

After she got word one night that the house of an African-American family had been firebombed for moving into an all-white neighborhood, she called the mayor at 2:00 a.m. Hofheinz and the chief of police went out to the site. The perpetrator was arrested that day.

Christia V. Daniels Adair

The first interracial political organization came about
when wealthy socialite Frankie Randolph called Christia at
the NAACP office to ask Christia's help in putting a stop to
the practice of "buying votes." Unscrupulous candidates gave
poor people favors, often in the form of liquor, to get their
votes. That interracial meeting resulted in the formal organization of the Harris County Democrats in 1953. Christia
compared the diversity at the meeting to a League of Nations
and credited the interracial group for Houston having less
violence during desegregation than other southern cities.

After she stepped down as head of the Houston
NAACP, Christia was asked to work in the Harris County
absentee voting office. She was the first African American
to work there, and the white women didn't know how to
react. The following week, the supervisor asked the workers
to bring in other volunteers. Christia brought in two African Americans, one white, and one Mexican woman.

Voting was supremely important to her. For twenty
years, she was judge for Precinct 25 in Houston's Third
Ward and proud that 85 percent of her precinct voted
in elections. In her eighties, she was hospitalized with a
broken knee but kept after the staff until they let a minister take her in a wheelchair to vote. The month before she
died, men from the Harris County Commissioner's office
came to her house and carried her to vote. One colleague
commented, "The thing that made her mad the most, just
outraged her, was when she'd look back at all the things she
did and then find out some people still don't vote."[21]

Linda L. Black's doctoral thesis compared the community leadership of Christia Adair and wealthy philanthropist Ima Hogg, daughter of a Texas governor. As a school board member, Hogg pushed for music programs and mental counselors for Houston children. Her passion for collecting led her to leave her River Oaks mansion as a museum of early American furnishings. Christia Adair had none of the advantages of wealth or social position but left a legacy of civil rights action that impelled Houston to create a public park in her name, featuring a mural of her life created by African-American folk artist John Biggers. As diverse as these two women were—literally the difference between black and white—their accomplishments were cut from the same mold. Both valued education, exhibited highly developed leadership skills, and assumed that they would succeed. And both left a legacy of service to their community.

At her death on December 31, 1989, at the age of ninety-six, Christia Adair performed one last act of public service. A note posted on her bedroom wall instructed the person who came to pick up her body that it was to be donated for science. "I want to be totally used up when I die serving mankind."[22]

FRANKIE CARTER RANDOLPH

Frankie Carter Randolph was a "rebel with a cause." Born in 1894, daughter of an East Texas lumberman, she showed her independent streak early. After the Carter family became wealthy and moved to Houston, she attended public and private school, but kept leaving schools when she became bored. She was arrested at fifteen for wearing her brother's gun and holster while riding horseback in Houston's Hermann Park. The Baptist church dismissed her for dancing.

She studied in Europe and in 1918 married Robert D. Randolph, a World War I pilot and later Houston banker. The couple had two daughters. With wealth at her disposal, she was prominent in equestrian circles and social groups—a founder and early president of the Houston Junior League. She was active in the League of Women Voters and charities. Actively involved in social causes, she volunteered at the Social Service Bureau and worked on issues of public housing and better drainage in poor sections of Houston. She was the first white member of the National Association for the Advancement of Colored People (NAACP) in Houston.

In 1952, she donated one thousand dollars to Adlai Stevenson's presidential campaign and was incensed when the Texas governor led state Democrats to back Republican candidate Dwight Eisenhower. Her political goals included ending the poll tax and segregation. Using her own money, she published a liberal periodical. Over the objection of conservative Democrats, she was elected Democratic National Committeewoman from Texas.

She and Christia Adair founded the Harris County Democrats. By her own count she attended thousands of precinct meetings with the message: Organize. And she worked diligently, making phone calls and writing letters. She counted liberal US senators and federal justices among her friends.

One observer commented that she was as comfortable at a precinct meeting in a black neighborhood as a dinner at the River Oaks Country Club. She moved in circles of power but was passionate about correcting social inequality. Politicians knew and feared her. She was outspoken, blunt, honest, and had more political power than any other woman in Texas in the 1950s. She died in 1972.

Lorraine Rey Isaacs Hofeller

1896–2002

Four-year-old Lorraine Isaacs huddled in her mother's lap through the night of September 8, 1900. Outside, a hurricane with howling wind and crushing storm surge battered Galveston, Texas. When the long night ended, the Isaacs' house still stood, but much of the city was a jumble of broken boards and destroyed buildings. Galveston Island had experienced what was until then the deadliest hurricane in American history. Lorraine Isaacs Hofeller, who died at the age of 106, remembered that day vividly. She was the last known survivor of the Great Galveston Storm.

Galveston Island is one of a chain of sand bar islands along the Texas coast. It is twenty-seven miles long and only three miles across at its widest point. It barely rises above sea level. Its highest point at the time of the storm was only eight and a half feet above sea level.

The city of Galveston, founded shortly after the Texas Revolution, became an entry point for immigrants in the mid-1800s. It prospered as its port hummed with activity, exporting cotton, hides, pecans, and other produce while importing goods from around the world. Lorraine's father, Benjamin David Isaacs, was a successful produce broker.

Lorraine was born in Galveston on February 24, 1896. She was a second-generation islander because her mother, Belle Isaacs, had been born there after Lorraine's grandfather emigrated from Alsace. Lorraine's birth gave the Isaacs a daughter to join their six-year-old son Mortimer.

By the time Lorraine was four, Galveston's thirty-six thousand residents made it the largest city in Texas. As the nation's leading port for exporting cotton, its citizens were among the wealthiest per capita in the nation. The Strand, Galveston's main commercial street, was called the "Wall Street of the South." Successful businessmen built huge mansions. Tall spires graced magnificent churches. Citizens enjoyed bookstores, lectures, debates, and theater performances. The resplendent Opera House had been built two years before Lorraine was born.

Lorraine's home, a two-story Victorian house at 2012 Broadway, had been constructed ten feet off the ground. Fourteen steps led up to the first floor. Its high perch away from the beach and its location on one of the higher parts of Galveston helped the house survive the 1900 hurricane.

Hurricanes, or "blows" as Lorraine called them, are common occurrences in the Gulf of Mexico. The word *hurricane* is almost exactly the same as the Spanish word *huracan*, which in turn comes from Hurakan, the name of the storm god of the Taino and Carib tribes that the Spaniards first met in the Caribbean.

These violent storms take shape in the warm waters of the Atlantic and the Gulf of Mexico. Today, television projections indicating landfall clearly show the northwest-erly direction of a hurricane's path, although it can make a curve to the east. The storms occur anywhere in the Gulf of Mexico and along the United States's eastern seaboard, but not on the West Coast. Although some may form in the waters near southern California, their westerly direction takes them far away from land. Those that approach Lower California are weakened by cooler Pacific water.

Hurricanes form anytime from late June through November, but the largest number of them occur in Sep-tember. The massive one Lorraine remembered came ashore the night of September 8, 1900. It had no name.

For more than a hundred years, people living in the Caribbean named a storm for the saint day in the Roman Catholic liturgical calendar the day of its occurrence. Later, the US began to identify storms by latitude/longiture desig-nations, but these were hard to read and easy to get wrong, so during World War II, meteorologists working in the Pacific began to use women's names to make them easy to remem-ber. This method was so simple that the National Hurricane Center adopted it in 1953, and weather forecasters began using the names of their girlfriends or wives as a joke. Now male and female names alternate in each year's list.

Names for some early hurricanes were assigned after a storm had passed and identified the place or object where the most damage occurred. The 1900 Galveston Storm etched in Lorraine's memory took its name from the city that sustained the full force of the storm. It sprang to life in

the Atlantic on August 27 as a disturbance, then passed over
Cuba as a tropical storm on September 3, raking Florida two
days later. The US Weather Bureau issued a bulletin about a
storm, but the report of Florida damage carrying a dateline
of September 7 did not appear in the *Galveston Daily News*
until the next morning—the day it struck the city.

A day earlier, beachgoers enjoyed the swells coming in
from the southwest. The sky was mostly sunny. That evening
was warm and pleasant with a full moon. A persistent sea
breeze provided comfort as Lorraine's family sat outside
on iron benches, greeting friends and relatives. Unknown
to them, the storm had intensified and was moving rapidly
northwest through the Gulf of Mexico. With no up-to-the-
minute information available, Galveston citizens found no
reason to be alarmed.

The person who *was* paying attention was Isaac M.
Cline, Galveston's local forecast official. He and his brother
Joseph, also a meteorologist, took readings on their instru-
ments—a barometer that measured atmospheric pressure
and an anemometer that measured wind speed. No visual
signs of an approaching storm were apparent, but the
eighteen-year veteran weatherman became cautious when
barometer readings began to fall, an indication a storm
could be approaching.

Heavy swells enjoyed by beachgoers that afternoon continued all night causing an unusually high tide. By 5:00 a.m.
the next morning the tide was overflowing low parts of the
city, and Cline telegraphed the weather Central Bureau in

Washington. Never before had he witnessed a tide this high with the wind pushing from the opposite direction.

The morning of September 8 was partly cloudy, and everyone went about their business as usual. About mid-morning, showers began. Lorraine and her mother were at a neighbor's house a block away. While Lorraine played with her doll, Mrs. Isaacs helped her friend pack for a trip to consult a doctor in New York City. Then it began raining in earnest. Since they had not brought an umbrella, they took the short way home through the alley. Mrs. Isaacs was surprised to find water where they were walking, much more water than the rain could have caused. It was the storm surge already overrunning the island.

Mr. Isaacs and ten-year-old Mortimer had come home for lunch. As the rain intensified, water rose, and Mortimer brought their dog inside. By that time the two bridges to the mainland were under water, cutting off any chance for escape.

The Cline brothers, increasingly alarmed over falling barometric pressure, set storm flags flying and went around town issuing warnings for people to take shelter in stronger buildings. By 3:30 p.m. half the streets in town were under water. At 6:00 p.m. the wind had increased to one hundred miles an hour and blew away the weather station's anemometer. The Category 4 hurricane had reached Galveston, and the worst was still to come as rain, wind, and storm surge continued to increase.

Houses broke apart. Some people fled to churches only to be crushed when the buildings collapsed. Roof and building timbers sailing like paper through the streets struck and killed many as they tried to find safer shelter. Rushing water picked up broken buildings, and the surge sent moving debris into action as a battering ram, destroying anything in its path. The roof of the Opera House caved in. The two bridges to the mainland were swept away.

About fifty people took shelter at Isaac Cline's home, a strong structure built about five feet above any previous storm water height. At 7:30 p.m. the weatherman was standing at his front door with eight inches of water in the house when, before he could turn around, water rose another four feet. It continued to rise until 8:00 p.m. when it reached a depth of fifteen feet. Rushing storm surge sent debris from ruined houses smashing into the Cline home. The house collapsed, killing eighteen people including Mrs. Cline. Isaac and his brother Joseph managed to grab hold of the three Cline daughters and were swept along on the floating mass. For three hours the men shielded the girls with their bodies, using planks to protect their backs from deadly projectiles. Near midnight the water began falling, and they finally came to rest about five blocks from where they started. Other survivors had been blown to the mainland across the bay.

The mass settled into a jumble of boards, furniture, and appliances twenty feet high. Trapped underneath were the living and the dead. It would be over a year before the last body was recovered and identified. Many would never be found. The area on the beach side of the debris was scraped clean all the way to the Gulf.

People had obeyed the warning to leave the beach, but the Sisters of Charity cared for ninety children at St. Mary's Orphanage right on the beach. They moved the children to the girls' dormitory, the newest and strongest building. As the storm grew more intense, the nuns began to sing an old French hymn "Queen of the Waves" to calm the children. Water entered the building, and they moved to the second floor. As it continued to rise, the ten nuns each tied six to eight children to themselves with a rope, hoping to save them. Some older children climbed on the roof. When the surge lifted the building off its foundation, the first floor collapsed and the roof caved in. Three boys survived by clinging to a tree, floating for hours before coming to land. All others were lost. The nuns and children were buried where they were found, still tied together.

The Isaacs were spared these horrors. During the fifteen hours the storm raged, they took refuge in the windowless dining room. Glass over the front door shattered, and Lorraine's father used a hammer to nail a rug over the opening to keep out the rain. A century later, Lorraine had not forgotten that night. "I remember sitting with my family at the dining room during the storm, with the blinds shut, not being able to see anything outside."[23]

Lorraine was scared, and she knew her mother was too. "I could tell my father was nervous because he kept walking back and forth all night."[24]

The next morning, the storm had passed. The Gulf was once again calm. After devastating Galveston, the storm tracked due north over the Great Plains before turning east across the Great Lakes, New England, and southern Canada. It finally disappeared over the Atlantic on September 15, leaving death and destruction along its path.

The Isaacs accessed the damage to their house. Lorraine followed her father upstairs to inspect the second floor. In one bedroom, the ceiling was bulging down. "My father took his walking cane and punched a hole through it, and all the water came down, and it scared me to death."[25]

But their house survived and so did they. More than six thousand others Galveston residents did not. The real number would never be known. Over thirty-five hundred houses were completely destroyed, with every house in town having some damage. In addition, churches and businesses sustained heavy damage.

The nation responded to the disaster. Seventy-eight-year-old Clara Barton arrived with the American Red Cross to help with the relief effort. Contributions poured in from around the nation and even foreign countries.

At Congregation B'nai Israel where the Isaacs were members, thirty-nine-year-old Rabbi Henry Cohen sprang into action. Many houses of worship had been completely destroyed, but the synagogue had received much less damage. Its doors were opened for other faiths to hold services. As ships began arriving with supplies, the rabbi drove through the city in a mule-drawn wagon to deliver food and medical supplies. As a recognized community leader, Rabbi Cohen was chosen to serve on the Recovery Committee that engineered the rebuilding of the city where he would serve his congregation for another fifty years.

With the city in such dire straits, Lorraine's mother took both children to Dickinson on the mainland. They stayed with relatives for a short time while Mr. Isaacs helped with the recovery.

To ensure city safety from another hurricane, the Recovery Committee initiated a two-pronged plan. The first was to build a sea wall as suggested by weatherman Cline. They hired three engineers including Henry M. Robert, better known for Robert's Rules of Order that govern meetings. The engineers recommended building a seventeen-foot-high concrete barrier to hold back storm surge. This led to the construction of a seawall built with forty interlocking concrete sections sunk into the beach. Originally it was three and a half miles long but soon extended to ten miles. The seawall remains intact today, although in 2008 Hurricane Ike was so wide that sea water went around the ends and pooled behind it, sparking plans to extend it even farther.

The second operation raised the town's elevation so that flooding would not be so costly. Fifty city blocks of homes and buildings were lifted by jacks so that sand from the Gulf could be pumped underneath. Structures that couldn't be raised had lower floors filled with sand. Lorraine remembered the constant sound of motors working as the land was built up. The height of the fill matched the top of the seawall and acted as a brace. Then the land sloped lower toward the port.

Six months after being dealt such a blow, recovery was well under way, but Galveston lost its premier place among Texas cities. Houston became the dominant port after dredging a fifty-mile ship channel to the Gulf of Mexico to accommodate ocean-going vessels.

But the city of Galveston did not die. Lorraine attended the 1911 opening of the upscale Galvez Hotel, built across the street from the seawall. Two years later, she was a senior at Ball High School. In a time when women had no voice in politics, she ran for class president and entered a debate with four boys for the position. Her platform was women's suffrage. She won and became the first young woman to be president of the senior class at her school.

Four years later, the United States entered World War I. Lorraine's brother Mortimer entered the Air Force and was stationed at an airstrip on Lake Worth. He became friends with Sigmar Kaiser Hofeller, also stationed in Fort Worth as a member of the US Army Signal Corps. Mortimer introduced Sigmar to his sister.

The war ended in November 1918, and two months later, on January 9, 1919, Lorraine and Sigmar married. They moved to Sigmar's hometown, Buffalo, New York, and during the next five years, daughters Marion and Elaine were born there. In 1934, though, the family returned to Texas and settled in Houston where Sigmar sold insurance for many years.

After Sigmar's death in 1964, Lorraine remained in Houston for the rest of her life. In 1975, as part of oral history files at Congregation Beth Israel where she was a member, she recorded her memories. Until the age of ninety-four, she continued to drive her car in the nation's fourth largest city.

Lorraine lived long enough to see Galveston return to prominence along the Gulf coast. Beaches and lively entertainment such as Mardi Gras became top tourist attractions. Performances returned to the restored 1894 Opera House. The tall ship *Elissa*, rebuilt for the US Bicentennial, permanently docked at the harbor that had once been her port of call.

Lorraine retained her ability to recall details of the storm. She likened her mind to kitchen cabinets, opening different doors and pulling out the memories. During the city's centennial celebration of the Great Galveston Storm, Lorraine received the key to the city. "It feels wonderful to be celebrating the storm's 100th anniversary. I never dreamed that I would be the last one."[26]

She spent her last six years in a Houston nursing home. On her wall hung a needlepoint picture of the house where her family survived the storm. She had created it from an old photograph. On the table she kept one of the little shoes she wore that night.

Lorraine Isaacs Hofeller died July 16, 2002. Hurricanes were the only thing that ever frightened her, but she never lost her love of Galveston. She is buried in the city where she was born.

GALVESTON'S COLORFUL CHARACTERS

Prior to the coming of Spanish explorers, Galveston Island was occupied by Akokisa Indians part of the year as they dug for clams. Heat and humidity made the area a perfect breeding ground for mosquitoes. The Indians smeared mud on themselves to escape swarms of the pesky insects.

The first recorded mention of the place generally considered to be Galveston Island came from Álvar Núñez Cabeza de Vaca in the early 1500s. He was second in command of an expedition seeking gold in Florida and sent a report of their activities to Spanish king Charles V.

The Spanish ships reached the Caribbean where they experienced a hurricane, a phenomenon unknown in Europe. After meeting disaster in Florida, 250 survivors set out in a makeshift flotilla toward Mexico but were shipwrecked on the Gulf coast. Eight years later, the remaining four survivors of the expedition walked into Mexico City. Cabeza de Vaca's report to the king detailed their tribulations.

Three hundred years later pirate Jean Lafitte chose the natural harbor on the north side of Galveston Island as a base for raiding Spanish ships. Fine china and elegant items taken from the Spaniards filled his "Red House" at the compound he called Campeche. When the US Navy forced Lafitte to leave the Gulf of Mexico, he burned Campeche and sailed away in his favorite ship *The Pride*. Nothing was heard of him again. Only rumors of buried treasure remain.

Shortly after Lafitte left, the 1836 Texas Revolution made the island part of the fledgling republic. The Galveston City Company was formed, and eccentric inventor Gail Borden began selling lots on the newly laid out streets of the town located at the east end of the island. By mid-century Borden had won an award in Europe for his meat biscuit, a dried patty of broth and flour useful for explorers and pioneers but so unappetizing that no one bought it. He placed a sail on a wagon, and his terraqueous [land/water] machine moved well on the hard-packed beach but dumped out the passengers once it hit the water. He lost a fortune trying to condense milk so it would not spoil. After moving to New York, he finally perfected the process and founded the Borden Milk Company.

HALLIE CRAWFORD STILLWELL (1897–1997)
COURTESY OF HALLIE CRAWFORD STILLWELL/TXDOT CRAWFORD

Hallie Crawford Stillwell

1897–1997

*N*obody would ever question that Hallie Stillwell had grit. Some of it may have come from the sand on the arid, thorn-infested Stillwell Ranch in the Big Bend of Texas where she ranched for so long. But nobody questioned her spunk. Not only did the former schoolteacher work alongside her husband in the grueling work of running the ranch, she raised three children, and later became a news columnist, lecturer, justice of the peace, and book author. It's easy to see why she became a legend in her one-hundred-year lifetime.

Hallie Crawford, eldest of Alvin Guy and Nancy Montgomery Crawford's five children, was born in Waco, Texas, on October 20, 1897. The Crawford family moved often as they sought a better life for their family and good education for their children.

At age three Hallie survived typhoid fever while the family was living in Ozona. At seven, she contracted diphtheria while they were in San Angelo. In the space of twelve years, the family made five moves, including a short stay in New Mexico.

Even though her mother insisted on genteel manners, Hallie was a tomboy, always preferring to be outside. She left housework and cooking to her sisters. When she was thirteen, the family was on the move again with Hallie and her sister driving the covered wagon to a new home in Alpine, Texas. Here, their father opened a grocery store.

Hallie entered sixth grade in Alpine and graduated high school in 1916. At age nineteen, after completing six weeks of training that summer at the Normal School for Teachers, now Sul Ross State University, she passed the state examinations and had a certificate to teach in Texas.

When a teaching position opened in Presidio about eighty miles south, she applied for the job. Presidio is an isolated town on the north bank of the Rio Grande about 120 miles upstream from the southernmost tip of the Big Bend area of Texas.

Just across the bridge in Mexico is Ojinaga, Chihuahua. Frequent changes in governments following the 1910 Revolution brought chaos to Mexico. Areas in northern Mexico along the Rio Grande became lawless. Although American soldiers were stationed at Presidio, raids by bandits like Pancho Villa disrupted life on both sides of the river. Hallie's father was particularly upset that she would choose to go to such an unsafe place. "Daughter, I think you are going on a wild goose chase."

Hallie responded with a flippant "Then I'll gather my geese." The phrase would become the title of her memoirs.[27] Her father sent her off with his six-shooter for protection.

Teaching in Presidio was the first test of Hallie's grit. She had been reared to be a southern lady, mindful of manners and appearance. The heat, sand, and spartan living conditions were a trial, but another woman teacher was there too. After Hallie's sister joined them, life became more tolerable. By her own words, "I was not a quitter."[28] She would prove that many times throughout her life.

Life was never boring, although it could be unsettling. Sometimes at night the women heard Mexican families driving their creaking carts through the town, seeking safety from border raiders. Notorious Pancho Villa often crossed the Rio Grande in this area and got the blame for all the pandemonium whether he actually caused it or not.

Life was pretty routine. In addition to teaching classes and cleaning the schoolhouse, the three women visited with Texas Rangers and customs agents in the evening and attended church on Sunday. Once a week they watched a silent movie.

The following year, to her parents' relief, Hallie left Presidio and took a teaching position in Marathon about thirty miles east of Alpine. Her family was much happier to have her closer to home and in a safer place.

She boarded with a family in Marathon, and one day a handsome friend of the family drove up in his Hudson Super-6 car. Hallie was impressed with tall, taciturn Roy Stillwell . . . and his car. They attended a Saturday night dance and kept dancing until the sun peeked over the mountains. Roy, twenty years her senior, began courting

Hallie. He took her for rides in the car, sent her candy, and even hired a fiddler and guitar player to serenade her. She sometimes woke up in the night to the sound of "Listen to the Mockingbird" being sung outside her window.

The Crawfords did not approve of the courtship. Besides the age difference, Roy had been married before and was known to drink and gamble at times. In spite of her parents' objections, on July 29, 1918, Hallie and Roy drove to Alpine in the Hudson and married anyway. The Crawfords finally warmed to their new son-in-law because he obviously cared for Hallie. Roy was honest and a respected rancher with a large spread. Hallie knew her father had secretly approved when he gave her his silver spurs that she wore for the rest of her ranching days.

Hallie went as a bride to a one-room bachelors' cabin on the Stillwell Ranch. The sparsely furnished room Roy shared with three hired hands did not even have a bed, only a bedroll on the floor. The hired hands, banished to the barn, took a dim view of her arrival. As Hallie walked to the cabin, she overheard one of them remark that she wouldn't last six months. They were wrong. Hallie Stillwell toughed out those initial surprises and inconveniences. The ranch would be a place of comfort to her all of her life.

The twenty-two-thousand-acre Stillwell Ranch was located forty-five miles south of Marathon near today's north entrance to Big Bend National Park. The Rio Grande was just twenty-two miles as the crow flies. In the unsettled conditions along the border, Roy would not let

Hallie stay at the ranch alone when the men left each day to work the cattle.

Hallie knew how to ride and had no qualms about riding with the men, but that first day was not without incident. Hallie's mother had made her a split skirt for riding, but when she tried to mount her horse, the skirt got caught on the saddle. It took her husband and the hired men to help her dismount from the bucking horse. Nobody spoke of the incident again, but Roy found a pair of men's pants for her to use as she shouldered work alongside the men, learning the cattle business hands on. Even her sunbonnet had to go in favor of a Stetson because the bonnet restricted her view. She refused however to give up the kid gloves that protected her hands. She even continued putting on makeup each morning, causing an impatient Roy to ask whether she thought the cows would notice.

Handling cattle was far different from horseback riding for pleasure. She felt awkward trying to do the unfamiliar tasks and humiliated when she was unable to do them satisfactorily. Roy gave few directions. His family had been cattlemen; he seemed to expect her to know what to do. Often, at the end of a particularly frustrating day, she was upset with herself for letting him down. The first time it happened, she walked in back of the cabin and sat on a sand dune staring across the river at the mountains in Mexico. Time and again, at the end of a long day working cattle, she went to sit on the sand dune "looking into the far-away beautiful mountains in Mexico and enjoying the lovely evening shadows so typical of West Texas at dusk. My emotions were calmed and I felt peace and happiness."[29] That view would be her solace for the rest of her life.

At the ranch one of the hired hands did most of the cooking to Hallie's joy, but she had much to learn even at the cabin—like the day she energetically scrubbed the old black coffeepot until it shined and erased ranch records when she washed the walls. It was months before the comments stopped.

She was grateful when Roy built an arbor across the front of the cabin. She planted honeysuckle and other vines to block the sun. This shady spot became her living room where they could sit in the cool of the evening. When she was away from the ranch, she was always eager to return. "I swore that I would never forsake that ranch."[30]

The Stillwells owned a house in Marathon, and they used it when they needed to be in town. They went there to await the birth of their first child. When the boy arrived in 1919, Roy called him Son, and the child was in the first grade before he knew that his real name was Roy Walker Stillwell. Elizabeth Marie was born the following year, and Son, trying to say "Baby," called her "Dadie." The name stuck. Two years later, Guy was born.

Hallie had help when the children were small, and this allowed her to return to ranch work with her husband. Because there was never a large enough crew, everybody pitched in. The children were all riding horses by the time they were three. Son shadowed his father everywhere.

He was large for his age and a strong worker. Guy was very sickly as an infant and often tired, but he was fine on horseback. Dadie liked being in the kitchen, something that never appealed to Hallie.

Roy needed every hand he could get. There was always so much to do on the ranch. Hallie learned to rope, tie, brand, round up cattle, mend fences, or whatever else needed to be done. The work was endless.

When the children reached school age, Hallie stayed with them in town during the school term. She became active in the Parent Teachers Association. When school trustee elections came, Hallie and another woman became the first women elected to the Marathon school board. She joined a civic group and spearheaded a project to save the town's first schoolhouse and was proud when the renovated building became the community center. That restoration project was actually a turning point, sparking her interest in history and historical places that lasted the rest of her life.

In the 1930s Big Bend began to be developed from a state park into a national park. Hallie was curious to see the progress. She and a friend made a visit. The man in charge told her he did not know how to get enough wood for the fireplaces in the cabins since the park did not allow trees to be cut. When she learned that the government would pay eighteen dollars for each cord of wood, Hallie jumped on the opportunity to earn some money. She told the park manager she would furnish the wood, cut into eighteen-inch lengths as specified. She had no idea how big a cord was and had to ask Roy. He described a cord of wood as a stack measuring four-by-four-by-eight feet. They hired Mexican men to cut the wood on the ranch, and Hallie was in business until the park put in oil stoves some years later.

Expenses grew as the children got older, and she opened a beauty parlor in her home in Marathon. She missed being at the ranch, though, and every weekend and holiday during the school year, she and the three children drove forty-five miles back to the ranch. Being there meant hard work, but in the evening, she found peace gazing out to the distant hills. The ranch was home.

Roy had two close calls with death. Hallie nursed him through tuberculosis, but he barely recovered from that before developing acute appendicitis. Neither time did the doctor think Roy could survive, but Hallie stayed at his side through both scary incidents, amazed at his will to survive.

Hard times came as dust storms blew in, sapping the life out of the ranch. Cattle grew weak from lack of water and grass. The prolonged drought caused ranchers to take government payment of twelve dollars a head to destroy cattle that had no hope of surviving. Hallie stood with tears in her eyes as bullets mowed them down.

Son graduated from high school in 1937 and returned to the ranch. Roy saw no need for the boys to go to college. He wanted them to learn ranching the way he had, by experiencing it. Dadie went to a boarding school in El Paso for high school, then graduated from Our Lady of the Lake College in San Antonio.

Two rooms had been added to the cabin after the arrival of the children, but Roy saw no need for modern conveniences. Hallie figured out ways to get a sink installed and contracted for the delivery of a butane-run refrigerator. Roy thought this was totally unnecessary until he found he had cold lemonade to drink in the hot summer. Hallie wanted to replace the outhouse with a bathroom, but he balked. She sawed lumber and built it anyway, "borrowing" better lumber from a fence the men were putting in.

War in Europe seemed far away until Pearl Harbor was bombed. Son and a friend announced they were going to join the Air Force and become pilots. Both topped six-five and were rejected because they wouldn't fit into the pilot's seat, but they remained in service. Son spent three years overseas, his letters a precious lifeline to his parents.

Rain, never abundant, seemed to dry up completely, and then came unexpected tragedy in 1948. Roy had gone into town for a load of hay. On the way home, the truck rolled over. He never regained consciousness and died of massive internal injuries. Roy often went for spells without speaking because it didn't seem necessary, but Hallie realized as she sat with him at the hospital that this silence was permanent.

She and her sons hung on to the ranch in face of severe odds. As the drought worsened, friends who were shipping their cattle to Colorado where there was grass and water advised them to do the same. As each load of cattle left the Stillwell Ranch, Hallie felt another part of Roy being torn

117

away from her. Then as the last truck headed toward the gate, rain began to fall. Hallie frantically yelled for the truck to stop. The driver returned to the cattle pens. Hallie stood in pouring rain, watching as the cattle entered the gate. Stillwell Ranch was still in business.

Times were hard, but she refused to let the ranch go under. To earn money, she gave lectures around the state. In 1956, she started a Ranch News column that ran in the *Fort Worth Star Telegram*, the *El Paso Times*, the *San Angelo Standard Times*, and *San Antonio Express*. She also was a reporter for United Press International and Associated Press. Two years later she and Virginia Madison co-wrote her first book, *How Come It's Called That?: Place Names in the Big Bend Country*.

Hallie continued to run the ranch until 1964 when she turned it over to her sons. That same year she was elected justice of the peace for Brewster County. She dealt out judgments and penalties for the 6,193-square-mile area with equity, even charging family members the maximum fine because she felt they should respect the law. She also officiated as coroner but got her greatest joy from performing weddings.

She held memberships in the West Texas Historical Society and the Brewster County Historical Society. She belonged to the Daughters of the Republic of Texas, United Daughters of the Confederacy, and the American Legion Auxiliary, as well as the Big Bend National Park and Development Committee.

Hallie Crawford Stillwell

Hallie published her memoirs, *I'll Gather My Geese*, in 1991. Before her death on August 18, 1997, just two months shy of her one hundredth birthday, she had completed ten chapters of the story of life after Roy's death. Her characteristic humor came out in the title she chose— *My Goose Is Cooked*. The book was completed by relative Betty Heath and published in 2004.

Honors came to Hallie Stillwell in many forms. She was a judge in the 1967 Terlingua Chili Cook-Off and the following year was designated permanent queen of the affair. Fifty years later, thousands of chili-heads still arrive each fall for the chili cooking competition and the raucous party associated with it at Terlingua, the desolate "wide place in the road" that once elected a goat as mayor.

Texas Parks and Wildlife magazine described her as a "tough-as-nails" cowgirl.[31] *Texas Monthly* named her "The Grande Dame of Texas." She was elected to the National Cowgirl Hall of Fame in 1992 and the Texas Women's Hall of Fame in 1994. The State Fair of Texas placed her in its 1998 Texas Hall of Honor that pays tribute to ranchers and farmers who have made significant contributions to the state. On a corner of the original Stillwell Ranch, she even had her own Hallie Stillwell Hall of Fame Museum next door to the Stillwell Store and RV Park. Although the ranch was sold in 2013, new owners continue to operate the store and museum with memorabilia related to Hallie Stillwell, a woman with grit and a true Texas Legend.

PANCHO VILLA—HERO OR VILLAIN

Pancho Villa is probably the best known of all Mexican bandits. He was a guerrilla fighter who made up his own rules. Born José Doroteo Arango on June 5, 1878, he spent his youth working on his parents' farm. When his father died, he became the head of the household. After escaping imprisonment for shooting a man who was harassing his sister, he set his own rules from then on.

A small-time rustler, Arango joined the uprising against Mexican president Porfirio Díaz's harsh government. He quickly rose to the rank of colonel because of his fighting skill, but when the new government fell from power, he barely escaped execution and fled to the United States. Returning to Mexico, he began to build his legend. Charisma, superb horsemanship so admired by the population, and strong-arm tactics made him into folk hero Pancho Villa. As head of a military force that he called Division del Norte, he was intensely generous and loyal to the soldiers who followed him and unrelenting in opposition to anyone who stood in his way. Sometimes he joined other revolutionaries and sometimes opposed them.

His popularity rested in his "Robin Hood" image of helping the poor while fighting powerful government officials. Two disastrous defeats robbed his army of any effectiveness in Mexican politics, and he began a series of hit and run raids on both sides of the Rio Grande.

In an effort to stop incursions into the United States, the government sent General John J. Pershing to bring Villa to justice. The American army pursued the elusive Villa for nine fruitless months. Efforts to find him stopped when the United States entered World War I and Pershing was recalled to lead US Army troops in Europe.

In 1920 Villa accepted the Mexican government's offer for him to retire to a ranch near Parral, Chihuahua. He turned it into a military-style camp for his soldiers. Three years later, he was assassinated, perhaps on orders from the Mexican president.

Pancho Villa promoted his own image, starring as himself in a movie of his life filmed at his ranch. He granted interviews to reporters. Balladeers composed *corridos* to sing his praises in a struggle against oppression. Novels grew out of his story.

In real life, he was a ruthless bandit who took what he wanted, disrupting society, but to the poor he represented retribution for government abuses—a real folk hero.

Donna Edith Whatley McKanna

1899–1986

Donna Edith Whatley McKanna could have been poster child for the stereotypical Texan. She had horses, oil, airplanes, and a showplace home on her ranch. She was the first woman independent oil operator in West Texas. She was a very early member of the 99s, an association of women pilots whose first president was Amelia Earhart. Her grandmother was one of the first settlers in Scurry County, Texas. She may have had all the trappings of a stereotype, but Edith was more than that. She had traveled the world and was master of the art of ikebana, Japanese flower arranging. Many organizations benefitted from her generosity of money and expertise. And yet, she chose to spend the last half of her life in the West Texas county where she grew up.

Edith Whatley was born about 1899 on the family farm between Waco and McGregor in Central Texas. Her parents were Daniel and Elizabeth (Betty) Courtney Spenser

EDITH WHATLEY MCKANNA (1899–1986)
SCURRY COUNTY MUSEUM, SNYDER, TEXAS

Whatley. She claimed no one ever told her exactly which year she was born, but her tombstone carries the birthdate July 19, 1899.

When she was quite young, her parents moved to Scurry County where her family had owned land since Edith's grandmother, Mary McGregor Whatley, moved to the Fluvanna area in 1880, just four years after the county was formed. The county would not be officially organized until four years after the McGregors arrived.

Edith's uncle, Dougal McGregor, settled in the community of Light before 1900 and helped develop the community of Fluvanna, serving as Fluvanna's first postmaster. The small town sits on the edge of the Caprock Escarpment that marks the eastern edge of the Llano Estacado (Staked Plains). The drop from the table-top flat Llano Estacado to the rolling plains below varies from several hundred to one thousand feet along its jagged length running in a north-south line through the middle of the Texas Panhandle. The lower plains often have flat-topped mesas with the clearly visible white layer of limestone rock that has not eroded away.

Dan and Betty Whatley moved to a farm near Fluvanna when Edith was small, and she received most of her schooling in the tiny town. Ranchers and others living in sparsely settled areas of Texas often sent their daughters to schools founded by the Sisters of St. Mary of Namur. The nuns had come from Belgium and established schools in Waco, Dallas, Fort Worth, Denison, Sherman, and Wichita Falls between 1870 and 1900. The schools were known for their scholastic excellence as well as artistic and cultural training. These advantages assured children an exposure to learning and culture that they were not likely to get in tiny schools in isolated areas.

Edith attended two Texas schools founded by nuns. One, the Academy of the Sacred Heart in Waco, was a "school for young ladies in a rough-and-tumble Waco celebrated for its gun fights."[32] Waco's description probably came as a result of cattle drives that passed through the town on the Texas portion of the Chisholm Trail during this period. The day school was open to boys and girls through eighth grade, but girls in high school could board while studying there. Edith's attendance at Waco's Victorian-style buildings would have come in the 1910s. The school closed in 1946. She also attended the Academy of Mary Immaculate in Wichita Falls.

While Edith was in her teens, shallow wells had begun to produce oil in Texas. Her father, as well as her future husband, became involved in the oil boom in northwest Texas and in southern Arkansas in the early 1920s. It's likely she met James Everett McKanna through business connections between the two men.

Regardless of how they met, twenty-one-year-old Edith was in El Dorado, Arkansas, on February 23, 1921, where she married twenty-two-year-old James McKanna. El Dorado had been the scene of feverish activity for the past month after the Busey oil well's massive oil plume signaled the discovery of oil. Population of the county seat of Union County, Arkansas, swelled from four thousand residents to twenty thousand

During the following year, the couple traveled extensively as they followed oil discoveries. Edith spoke of driving miles of dirt roads in a Model T with her husband before they made their permanent home in Wichita Falls. They were in El Paso, Texas, when their daughter, Elizabeth Belle McKanna, was born. They called her Betty, the same as her Grandmother Whatley.

Edith began her flying career almost by accident. She was one of the earliest women to get her pilot's license. Her interest in flying began while she and her husband were in Europe. Edith, daughter Betty, and Betty's young friend accompanied James McKanna to Spain in 1929. While her husband remained in Spain on business, she and the girls went to London to take riding lessons on English hunters. Edith had some "nice" horses but no experience with jumping. She was eager to attend Smyth's Academy in London where she could take lessons from a well-known equestrian teacher.

When her husband finally arrived in London, he wanted Edith and the girls to fly to Paris with him. She had never been in an airplane, and it was quite disconcerting to see the attendant remove the door to bring their luggage aboard. It seemed all too possible that the door would come off during flight. Fortunately that did not happen, and the attendants in Paris took off both doors to remove their trunks, saddles, and golf bags. She pronounced it a very happy flight.

A family spat, however, occurred once they got home. James McKanna went to Wichita, Kansas, and bought a six-passenger Travel Air plane (now called a Beechcraft). She was not happy about his doing so because she did not want that plane to make her a widow. Nor did she see any reason to buy something as unnecessary as an airplane. But her attitude was about to change.

One Sunday soon after that, her husband took her to watch pilots barnstorming at a Wichita Falls airfield. Her husband's pilot encouraged her to go up in a bigger plane, just to see what it was like. She did and loved it—the whirr of the engine and the beautiful view of the countryside below. She was hooked and began taking flying lessons. She soloed in 1929, got her license the following year, eventually logging over three thousand hours flying.

Her flight test proved to be quite a surprise. When she and her husband arrived at the field, the flight instructor encouraged her to try out the new plane that was parked nearby. She accepted the challenge but it was a speed plane, and she felt it was just too fast, not so easy to handle. It took three tries before she was able to land. In her concentration on landing safely, she overlooked the note saying the plane was hers. Once they were on the ground, she was puzzled by her husband's look of disappointment. Then someone asked how she liked having her own plane! It was a perfect gift for her.

She described flying in those days. "We flew from 'dead reckoning' from a road map . . . Most pilots flew down the railroads or highways. Each town or area had its own special identification—a water tank, a church steeple, a granary, or some natural landmark that we pilots learned. . . . Later when the government sent me to school to learn navigation, I had a hard time passing. It was quite an ordeal for me to look at that map, work the compass, and hold the wheel to fly, all at the same time."[33]

Once she started flying, she sometimes flew to Fluvanna and landed in a field on her parents' farm. Her father chided her for scaring the mules and chickens when she came in low over the barn. But he couldn't say too much. He was an oil man and used a plane when he went to Wichita Falls on business. After her parents purchased the Cross C Ranch in Borden County, her father created a landing strip by covering up prairie dog holes. He would stand holding a sheet to let Edith know the direction of the wind when she flew there. Sometimes the wind was so strong the sheet wrapped around him.

Edith recalled flying out to the ranch with her younger sister Merle and young Betty. On the way they encountered a dust storm. During the 1930s enormous clouds of dust kicked up by winds over drought-stricken farms on the Great Plains, particularly the Texas Panhandle, western Oklahoma, and Kansas, blotted out the sun. Edith was flying over Haskell, Texas, hoping to get home to Wichita Falls, when she hit a cold front that Texans call a blue norther. The fierce north wind made it seem as if the plane had hit a brick wall. Air temperature dropped in an instant. They were all strapped in and wearing goggles, but they were bounced around so severely that Edith decided to land in a field nearby. The police arrived, along with townspeople. One woman was particularly upset and threatened to have them arrested until she realized something about the pilot. "Why, you're a woman! Oh, my! Birds are made to fly. Not women! Not men! Pray to the Lord."[34] The woman finally calmed down and no one was arrested.

It was not a plane crash that took James McKanna's life as Edith had feared. He suffered a fatal heart attack in May 1933 and died at age thirty-four. Burial was in Oklahoma City.

Edith remained active in the oil business, and she continued flying, something she would do until she was almost seventy. When World War II came in 1941, airplanes were in short supply, and she donated her plane to the war effort. In addition, she served three years at Air Force headquarters as liaison for the Air Force and the Civil Air Patrol (CAP). This civilian group had been formed as Nazi Germany stepped up its aggression. CAP planes watched for German U-boats in the Atlantic and the Gulf of Mexico. Initially the planes were unarmed and merely reported sightings. Later, they released depth charges against enemy submarines. CAP also provided patrols along the southern border of the United States. They trained pilots, transported cargo, and performed the rather precarious job of towing targets for antiaircraft gun practice. During the last two years of World War II, these tasks were performed by the Women's Airforce Service Patrol (WASP), who trained at Avenger Field in Sweetwater, Texas.

Following the war, Edith was in Japan several years during the time of the American occupation. While there, she developed an interest in ikebana, the Japanese art of flower arranging. She studied the style of ikebana called Saga Go-ryū, named for Emperor Saga who reigned in the ninth century. The Saga Go-ryū school occupies the former residence of the emperor in Kyoto, the ancient capital of Japan. Edith's study led to her designation as a master ikebana instructor. After she returned to the states, she maintained membership in Ikebana International and was in demand as a speaker at garden clubs and teacher of this exquisite style of flower arranging.

By 1949 Edith was back in Scurry County where she grew up. She became actively involved in the oil business, organizing the Imperial Oil Company and securing leases. Her discovery well, the Ossie Buffalo, came in on the Fuller field, making her the only woman oil operator in Scurry County's Canyon Reef field in the eastern edge of the massive Permian Basin oil reservoir. During the boom in 1949, she held leases on eighty-six thousand acres of land and had seven producing wells. She maintained a room at the Manhattan Hotel on the courthouse square in Snyder, Texas, to be near her office. She visited her rigs wearing smart suits, heels, hat, and white gloves to make sure the men knew that a lady was around. The February 21, 1949, issue of *Time* magazine mentions her in the article about Canyon Reef discoveries. Two years later she received a scroll of distinction from Vice President Alben Barkley recognizing her as one of seven of the Southwest's most distinguished women.

On Rock Ledge Farm, the Whatley property near Fluvanna, she inherited an old "shotgun" house. The term "shotgun" supposedly came from the fact that the house was one room wide, with the rooms arranged in a row in such a way that a person standing on the front porch could shoot a bullet out the back door without hitting a wall. With exquisite taste and the means to accomplish it, she remodeled the house into a showplace that provided an elegant setting for the wedding reception of the daughter of a friend. The house became the scene of business transactions between important oil executives. State and national political figures, even show business personalities, were entertained there.

Edith was active in Snyder during the time the county seat transformed from a quiet farming and ranching community to a thriving town. She served as chairperson of the Scurry County Historical Commission, and led in efforts to restore the historic Cornelius Dodson House, one of the oldest homes in the county, serving as chairperson of the furnishings committee. She was a director of the Snyder Country Club as well as a founder of the community meeting facility called the Martha Ann Woman's Club in memory of the daughter of a local oil man.

She was a leading benefactor of Western Texas College (WTC), Snyder's community college, and also the Scurry County Museum, situated on the WTC campus, donating the Japanese water garden in front of the museum. Edith maintained membership in the National Garden Club and was a life member of the Snyder Garden Club.

When the National Ranching Heritage Center (NRHC) was founded in Lubbock, Texas, she became a charter member of the Ranching Heritage Association that funded and supported the development of NRHC. The nineteen-acre outdoor museum contains more than forty early West Texas buildings associated with ranching. Edith aided substantially in restoring the historic Harrell House (ranch house) and furnished the parlor at the orientation center of the NRHC complex in honor of her parents.

While some might classify Edith McKanna as a stereotypical Texan, she put her individual spin on her time in the Lone Star State. She lived a life that spanned early aviation to the space age and was a member of the group of early women aviators. She maneuvered through the male-dominated world of the oil business to take her place as an independent businesswoman. She found beauty in exquisite ikebana arrangements and taught others this art. She generously gave time and money to preserve the ranch life she loved. When she died March 26, 1986, she chose to be buried in the tiny Fluvanna, Texas, cemetery at the edge of the Caprock overlooking the rolling Texas plains.

THE WOMEN PILOTS OF WORLD WAR II

In November 1929 a group of licensed women pilots met at Curtiss Field on Long Island to form an organization. One hundred seventeen women pilots were eligible at that time, and ninety-nine became charter members, sparking the name the 99s. Amelia Earhart was elected first president. The organization continues today with headquarters at Will Rogers World Airport in Oklahoma City, Oklahoma. They promote advancement in aviation through education and scholarships. Membership is open to any female pilot or student pilot with current certification. They own and maintain Earhart's birthplace in Atchison, Kansas, where they hold their annual reunion.

In 1939, as storm clouds gathered in Europe with Hitler's army advancing into Poland, record-setting pilot Jackie Cochran sent a letter to First Lady Eleanor Roosevelt detailing how women pilots could aid in case the United States went to war. Edith Love, another 99s member, had the same idea. Mrs. Roosevelt was enthusiastic and wrote about the idea in her newspaper column, "My Day." Most of the military, however, were skeptical—women had no place among the all-male group.

When the United States entered World War II two years later, women began to take traditional male jobs vacated by men called into service. A shortage of male pilots for non-combat flying occurred because so many had entered military service. In 1949 General "Hap" Arnold, commander of the Army Air Force, approved the training of women pilots to ferry military planes, and the Women's Airforce Service Pilots (WASP) came into being.

After training at Avenger Field in Sweetwater, Texas, WASP flew every type of aircraft the Army had. They ferried planes to bases and transported personnel and equipment. In addition, they flew test flights on repaired aircraft before men were allowed to fly them again. Still more harrowing, they towed gunnery targets.

During its two-year operation, WASP numbers reached 1,074, with thirty-eight of them dying in service-related accidents. General Arnold tried to get Congress to designate the WASP as members of the military, but that would not come until President Carter signed a law in 1977 granting military status. In 2009 President Obama awarded these women pilots the Congressional Gold Medal, the highest civilian award for achievements that impact American history.

The WASP spirit echoes that of Amelia Earhart, who left a note for her husband in case she did not return from her 1937 flight around the world. "Please know I am quite aware of the hazards. I want to do it because I want to do it. Women must try to do things as men have tried. When they fail, their failure must be but a challenge to others."[35]

Alma Pennell Gunter

1909–1983

Alma Pennell Gunter (pronounced Gunther) was born to be an artist. In a time when African Americans were still struggling to gain civil rights, she was trapped in the roles assigned to her race and gender during that era. And yet, art would be her solace when sadness overtook her life. From the depths of her memory, she created scenes from her childhood in vibrantly colored folk art.

Alma Pennell was born in Palestine, Texas, on June 11, 1909. Her mother was Flora Estelle Gardner Pennell. Her father, John Henry Pennell, worked for the railroad. The couple had six children. Alma was number three.

At a very early age Alma showed an interest in art. She loved to draw, but nobody encouraged her. When Alma was nine, the family moved to land outside the Palestine city limits because Mrs. Pennell wanted her children to be resourceful. On a farm the Pennell children could raise their own food and in the process supplement their father's wages.

Life was not easy for African Americans in the first half of the twentieth century in East Texas. Economically, they had little opportunity for employment other than that of servants or menial labor at very low wages. Socially, segregation was in full swing. Politically, they were discouraged from voting. During Alma's teen years, the Ku Klux Klan, organized to promote white supremacy in the South following the Civil War, had resurfaced in the guise of patriotism at the time of World War I. Its original purpose of suppressing African Americans had simply expanded to include hatred of Jews, Catholics, and immigrants or anybody who was not Caucasian.

When she reached her teens, Alma attended the all-black Lincoln High School in Palestine, graduating in 1927. No African American she knew even considered becoming an artist. Everyone was supposed to work and earn money. But Alma wanted more. "I knew I wanted to be an artist. . . . My mother wouldn't hear of it."[36]

Once she was out of high school, she continued to draw sketches of her surroundings. These would later appear in her painting, but it was useless to think she could earn enough money from her art to support herself at the time. She was forced into menial jobs, the only kind open to her. As a "domestic" worker, she cleaned houses and cooked. She earned money making clothes for other people. She worked as a hairdresser, and even spent a period of time washing dishes at the local cafe. These were jobs, however, not a career. Alma saw nursing as a better alternative, but that required education and training. So she worked and saved her money.

In 1936 she entered Prairie View College about fifty-five miles northwest of Houston. Founded in 1876 with

ALMA PENNELL GUNTER (1909–1983)

the name Alta Vista Agriculture & Mechanical College of Texas for Colored Youth, it trained teachers and industry workers at first but expanded a dozen years later to include arts, sciences, and nursing. Under the strict segregation system of the time that did not allow African Americans to attend classes with white students, this historically black school was a place for higher education where Alma could learn nursing. Its low tuition as a state school helped her manage costs. Forty years after Alma was there, the college was admitted into the Texas A&M University system. The 1876 Texas constitution had established the Permanent University Fund to provide support for higher education, but the funds were available only to the University of Texas and Texas A&M. Joining the Texas A&M system provided additional funding to expand the school's facilities and curricula. The college Alma attended now bears the name Prairie View A&M University. It remains a predominately African-American school with wide curriculum options open to students of any race.

Alma arrived at college determined to become a nurse, but she had not lost interest in art. With free time to spend as she pleased, she turned to the thing she had been denied so long. She ordered an art manual from Sears and Roebuck and bought a set of paints and brushes. Even though studying for academic subjects and fulfilling the student nursing requirements took much of her time, she still managed to create art on her own. There was no teacher. She just painted.

When she finally felt confident enough, she entered a campus art and poetry competition sponsored by the Dilettante Literary Society. She not only won, she repeated her first place showing the second year. Winning these competitions validated her as an artist and encouraged her to continue. Her grades did not suffer as a result—she graduated with honors in 1939.

After working for a time at the Prairie View college infirmary, she moved to Houston to work as a registered nurse at Jefferson Davis Hospital in Houston. The original Jefferson Davis Hospital on Elder Street was a stately classic four-story building built to care for Harris County indigents, but that is not where Alma would work. The old hospital had been replaced in 1937 by a new twelve-story art deco building on Allen Parkway, and the complex included housing for nurses. The new facility was the nation's first trauma research center and became a major maternity site—twenty-five babies were born during a twenty-hour period in 1960, long after Alma left Houston. The art deco building survived until May 15, 1999, when it was imploded on live television to make way for a four-story apartment complex. The fate of the original Jeff Davis Hospital would probably have pleased Alma much better. After being abandoned for many years, it found new life providing lofts for artists.

When Alma arrived in Houston in 1938, art was again shoved aside, and during the next twenty years she had little time for it. For the three years she spent at Jefferson

Davis Hospital, her days were filled with a heavy workload because many poor patients came for free treatment.

Then, World War II came in December 1941. Alma married C. C. Gunter and moved to Riverside, California, where her husband was stationed. Four years later they moved to San Francisco where he had been assigned. Alma continued her nursing career. Although the couple had no children of their own, Alma helped to raise her stepdaughter. There was little time for painting, but she experimented some with watercolors. She created church posters and made small portraits of her and her husband.

Alma's parents moved back into the town of Palestine, but since she lived on the West Coast, she was not able to see them often. The death of her father in 1960 affected her deeply, and she turned to art to help her deal with her grief.

Four years later, her husband lost his battle with cancer. She again found solace in art. "I could blunt the edge of pain and grief with a paint brush."[37] Around this time her stepdaughter married. Alma, who suffered from asthma, retired from the exhausting work of nursing in 1961. Free at last to paint, she was able to do the thing she loved.

She drew and painted, but there was no organization or system. She painted on paper and even the walls of her house in San Francisco. Tragedy struck again in 1970 when her sister, who had been taking care of their mother, died in a car accident. At sixty-one, Alma returned to Palestine, Texas, to take care of her mother and teenage nephew. She painted for her own therapy.

Four years later her nephew left for college, but her mother's health grew worse. Even though she spent most of her days caring for her mother, Alma was able to find the time to experiment with new media. She found inspiration in new books. The Palestine Negro Women's Business and Professional Club held an annual art show each year in February to celebrate Black History Month, and she entered five paintings in the 1978 exhibition.

The following month, during the annual Dogwood Trails tour, she entered a painting in the Palestine Art League's exhibit and won third prize in the folk art category. This led to her first sale when the president of the bank where the exhibition was held bought one of her paintings.

The following year she entered the Art League competition again, and this time took first place in the folk art category. This success was tempered by the loss of her mother. Alma, now seventy years old, chose to live alone. She was free to paint the scenes that she remembered from her childhood.

In 1980, she entered the Palestine Art League competition for the third time and won "best of show." Her art attracted the attention of a Dallas art collector who became her friend and promoted Alma's paintings. She had offers from different galleries to exhibit her paintings, but she chose instead Jack and Nancy Lockridge's gallery in Palestine. "I feel sentimental about . . . Palestine, about Texas, about the people, about my family, about my growing up here."[38]

Alma was deliberate about her work. She began a painting by making a pencil drawing on her sketchpad to lay out the general composition. She bought pre-stretched, primed canvasses and worked in acrylics because the solvent for oils aggravated her asthma. She gave the quick-drying acrylics credit for teaching her to mix colors. In many of her paintings her use of vibrant red, green, blue, turquoise, orange, and yellow colors in the foreground give a flattened appearance, but many small figures bring the scenes alive with action. While the paintings are highly composed, they accurately portray the story Alma wanted to tell.

After being told paintings with figures sell better, she put lots of them in her paintings. *Saturday Afternoon* reveals the bobbing heads of children splashing in the small stream. *Pretty Mama*, a dance hall scene painted in 1981, has twenty-seven figures including five dancing couples.

Although she lived under segregation, her paintings depict happy scenes from her childhood. "I paint what my mind photographed and recorded over all the years of my life."[39] She knew that these scenes from another era were things the modern world would never see and wanted to preserve them. They reflect her experience in Palestine's African-American community in the early twentieth century. The paintings are about everyday activities—wash day, kitchen activities, waiting for the ice man, a church funeral, and a baptism. "I can't put a label on it that says that it's 'black art,' although the people within my paintings are black . . . Since they are based on experiences that

I had as I was growing up they would just about have to be black."[40]

A painting called *Winter Cry* is a seemingly benign winter farm scene until you look closely and realize it shows hog-killing time. In the background the pig is being herded toward the pen where a man holding a sledgehammer waits to begin the process. In the foreground a woman holds a large knife with two more on the table. Nearby is a huge black pot over a blazing wood fire waiting to render the fat into lard. The title becomes clear when you realize the little girl racing out of the picture is holding her mitten-encased hands over her ears. "I ran into the house to keep from hearing."[41]

Another painting depicts lunch outside a country church holding all-day services. *Dinner on the Grounds* gave her statewide recognition when it was included in a two-year touring exhibition called "Texas Women—A Celebration of History." It features a remarkable thirty-one figures wearing Sunday clothes, each doing something different. People of all ages sit at the two large outdoor tables. Others sit under trees. A baby plays on a quilt while three children chase each other in the background. A solitary figure, perhaps the preacher, casts a long shadow from the doorway of the church. Alma had lived that scene.

Alma called some of her work "statement" paintings, ones where she explained the painting so the viewer would not miss the meaning. *The Haves and the Have-Nots* did not really need a statement—it showed African-American children staring in wonder as they walk through an affluent neighborhood. *Animals' Ark* is Noah's flood in reverse—the animals are aboard and the people on the shore. She wrote, "Would it not be justice in action if the 'flood' were to recur, and the animals given charge of the ark; and the humans—trying desperately to get on board—found themselves excluded?"[42]

Alma continued to paint until her death on May 14, 1983. Following her death, her art was included in a traveling exhibition sponsored by the Texas Folklife Resources and Austin's Laguna Gloria Art Museum. Exhibitions in Dallas in 1987 and 1988 displayed her work at the Museum of African American Life and Culture.

Once she started painting, Alma declined art lessons. She wanted her mind to guide her and not to be influenced by anyone else. Denied the opportunity to express herself with art as a child, adult Alma Gunter painted from her soul.

FOLK ART

Folk art, as opposed to fine art, is not created as "art for art's sake." It was primarily utilitarian or decorative, not created for beauty or esthetics as fine artists do. The colors used are usually strong, often vibrant. Many folk artists depict scenes of a former time, such as Alma Gunter did. These are actions and situations remembered by the artist.

This type of art is usually the creation of a particular culture, perhaps ethnic or even religious. The artists may be poor or working class persons with little education. Others may be educated but have had no exposure to art training. Without the benefit of learning how to create perspective, the artists' paintings appear flat. Objects may be out of proportion. Figures may look stiff and not be portrayed realistically. But there is no mistaking what the picture is about.

An alternate name for folk art is "naive art" because the artists have not been exposed to conditions that would influence their work. They usually learn from trial and error or perhaps through apprenticeships. That is not to say that a folk artist is not skilled. Some simply are able to reproduce the picture in their mind. Anna Mary Robertson Moses, better known as Grandma Moses, began painting scenes of rural farm life at age seventy-eight. *Sugaring Off* sold for over a million dollars.

Folk art encompasses more than just paintings on canvas or wood. Tole painting decorated wooden chairs or chests and metal utensils like coffee pots. Antique art such as weathervanes, old store signs, painted carousel horses, and carved wooden figures and scrimshaw are collector's items. Quilts, a particular form using geometric pieces, remains a popular craft today. And yes, street tagging, although it is a form of graffiti that is vandalism, is a form of folk art.

Annie Mae McDade Prosper Hunt

1909–2003

All Annie Mae Hunt ever wanted was for people to treat her with dignity. For a woman who lived through beatings by racists, grueling menial work for pennies a day, and the indignity of segregation, she never lost her spirit to take life on her own terms. Church, family, and friends were important, but she found her calling when she got involved in politics. Her efforts in getting people to vote paid off when she was able to attend the inauguration of President Jimmy Carter.

Annie Mae McDade was born August 29, 1909, in Washington County, Texas, near the little town of Wesley about thirteen miles southwest of Brenham. Her early years living near her grandparents were happy ones. Her grandmother, Matilda (Tildy) Boozie Randon, lived to be 101 and was a great influence in Annie Mae's life.

Tildy Boozie was born in South Carolina about 1846 while slavery was still in force. The name Boozie was probably a phonetic spelling of the name of the family that owned her.

Slaves had no rights, and there was no regard for slaves' feelings. They were simply property. If for some reason the owner needed money or had more slaves than needed, he sold them. There was no regard for breaking up families when individuals were sold to different owners.

Annie Mae's grandmother spoke of her bitter tears when her own mother was sold. Tildy's siblings had already been sold, and she never heard of any of them again. But Tildy was the Mistress's favorite. To stop the little girl from crying, she promised, "Don't worry, Tildy. I'll take care of you."[43] And she kept her promise. Tildy remained with them until emancipation. But that security came with a price.

By the time Annie Mae's grandmother was thirteen, the Boozie family had moved to Mt. Pleasant, Texas. Soon after that, the master's son raped Tildy. The Mistress threatened Tildy if she ever told anyone who the father was, but proof enough came when very light-skinned baby Theodore was born.

Tildy married Eli Randon, and the Mistress gave Tildy her own wedding dress to wear when she and Eli "jumped over the broom." Eli had an imposing physique and claimed to be a Seminole Indian. More than likely he was a Black Seminole, descended from southern slaves who escaped to Florida. The Seminoles allowed runaway slaves to live among them because they had skill as farmers and were valuable as interpreters since they could speak English. The group had their own leaders and a great degree of independence in exchange for giving a share of their crops to the Seminole.

ANNIE MAE MCDADE PROSPER HUNT (1909–2003)

TOMAS PANTIN, PHOTOGRAPHER

After Florida became part of the United States, Black Seminoles fought alongside the Seminole in a bitter resistance
against removal to Indian Territory. For the Black Seminole it
meant a return to slavery. After being forced into Indian Territory, bands of them escaped to Mexico and others scattered.

Tildy and Eli were married more than seventy-five
years and had sixteen children. The youngest was Callie,
Annie Mae's mother. The end of the Civil War brought an
end to slavery, and the Boozies gave Tildy fifteen hundred
acres of land in Washington County near Brenham, because
of Theodore.

Eli's name appears on a number of land transactions
in the Brenham area, but he called himself a preacher and
had a knack for leaving during the season of hard work and
returning when the cotton bales were ready to sell. His own
children and grandchildren were forced to work because he
was gone so much. Eli's land transactions were often unsuc-
cessful, and he lost much of Tildy's property.

Tildy became a skilled midwife, and women of both
races depended on her care during childbirth. Annie Mae
was never allowed to touch the satchel in which her grandmother carried the tools of her trade. Often Tildy stayed
a month with a white family helping do the wife's chores
and taking care of the baby. For this she earned about thirty
dollars, and when she came home, she brought white (light)
bread that Annie Mae gobbled down like candy.

Even though Tildy's house had no indoor plumbing
or electricity, Annie Mae's grandmother allowed no dingy

clothes. She made lye soap and soaked and boiled the clothes in big iron pots over a fire. Then the clothes had to be rinsed three times until the water was clear. When the well went dry in the summer, Annie Mae and her cousins had to carry water from the spring to fill their grand-mother's wash pots.

The conditions seem primitive by today's standards, but Annie Mae's grandparents were well off compared to other freedmen, and even some whites. They owned their house and land and even had sharecroppers living in houses Eli had built on the farm.

Callie, as the baby of the family, was her father's pet. When she was just sixteen, she eloped with George McDade. Her angry parents drove a wagon through the countryside for three weeks looking for them. Tildy sat with a shotgun across her lap to deal with the man who "stole" her baby. She never used it, however.

Annie Mae, favored grandchild of the favored daughter, was born when Callie was twenty. Annie Mae had an older brother and would later have a younger sister.

When her brother walked the seven miles to school, she tagged along even though she was not yet six, and the teacher let her stay. As she got a little older, she looked forward to the program the children put on at the end of the school session. Annie Mae and her sister were the star singers. Although she had a sharp mind, Annie Mae never got past fifth grade. She learned enough to read and write. Later in life she improved her skills by attending adult education classes.

Annie Mae's father left when she was seven, and her mother supported the three children alone—washing, ironing, chopping cotton, and cooking for a lumber camp. The next year, hoping for a better life, Callie took her children to Dallas, and they stayed there five or six years. Again Callie cooked, washed clothes, and chopped cotton. Annie Mae's brother swept out stores while Annie Mae and her sister together chopped weeds out of a cotton row. Because they were so young, the two of them together earned the same as one adult.

When the situation became desperate, Grandfather Eli showed up with money. He brought meat from hogs butchered on the farm and provided them with huge sacks of sugar, flour, and rice. Annie Mae, still a child, did not realize he was paying their rent and helping them get by when Callie's earnings simply were not enough to take care of the family.

Every summer as soon as school was out, Annie Mae went back to her grandparents' farm. She chopped weeds out of the cotton. Besides working in the cotton field, Annie Mae helped gather peanuts and peas for her grandparents to sell. Her grandmother sold milk and butter from the cows. But to Annie Mae, the huge watermelons were the best thing about being at her grandparents' farm.

When Annie Mae was about thirteen, her mother remarried and moved the family to Navasota in Grimes County. They had not been there but a few months when her stepfather said something that angered some white men. He ran away to avoid a beating, and the men came looking for him. Infuriated when they could not find him, they attacked the family. They broke Annie Mae's arm so that it never healed properly. They smashed her sister's nose with a pistol and beat her mother so badly that Callie could not walk for three months.

This was a time when the Ku Klux Klan was in full force in Grimes County. These men did not wear traditional Klan hoods, so Annie Mae knew who they were. Their tactics, however, were those of the Klan—beatings and hangings to intimidate African Americans. Law officers were often in sympathy with the Klan, but after the election of Miriam (Ma) Ferguson, Texas's first woman governor, the organization's activities declined. Racial prejudice, however, did not disappear.

Annie Mae dropped out of school after this traumatic event. In 1924, when she was fifteen, she married John Robert Prosper. About this time, her mother left the area and gave Annie Mae her sewing machine. The man who had brutalized Annie Mae's family demanded the sewing machine, but John Prosper refused to give it to him. Fearing what might happen to them, Prosper spoke to his white boss about the situation, and no retaliation came.

The marriage produced three children—Esther Mae, Dorothy Lou, and Doris Minola, but Prosper had a cruel streak. He and Annie Mae physically fought until finally she left with the children and went to Dallas.

After their divorce, she struggled to provide for her three children, and worked late into the night. She washed, cooked, and ironed, just as her mother had done. On a typical day Annie Mae earned fifty cents by working at two different houses. She got up before dawn, dressed her children while they still slept, made their lunches, then left a note for a kind neighbor, Big Mama, to come and wake them for school. There were times late at night when she went to sleep in the chair combing their hair and woke up to find the child asleep on the floor beside her.

Annie Mae had steady work at two houses, but sometimes she did as many as four washes a day. Her routine followed a pattern. At one house she washed clothes and hung them to dry, then went to the next house to wash and hang clothes. After that, she returned to the first house to iron, then went back to the second house to iron. She was proud of her ironing. "A fly couldn't stand on the collar."[44]

She also cooked supper for one family and then washed the dishes. This meant that sometimes she did not get home until after ten o'clock when dinner was late because the man of the house had not come home from work at the usual time. Her children had a key to get in their house, but in the summer Annie Mae might find her children asleep on the doorstep. She would see Big Mama sitting at the window next door, watching to see that they were safe until Annie Mae got home. "You don't need no *certain* somebody. You need *somebody*,"[45] she said. Years later, she took little presents to Big Mama because she had been the *somebody* Annie Mae needed to be able to work and support her children.

Annie Mae married again, this time to George Darden, and had her fourth child, George Washington Darden. The Dardens moved to Lubbock where they picked cotton and did odd jobs. After four years they returned to Dallas because Annie Mae hated the sand storms and the cold winters in the Panhandle. But in Lubbock she got a Social Security card, her first direct connection with government.

After the Dardens returned to Dallas, Annie Mae began a long employment with one family. When World War II started in 1941, wages began to rise. George Darden made ten dollars a day, and Annie Mae earned $8.50 a day doing housework and frying pies for a pie shop at night. Annie Mae also found that she was a good salesman for Avon products. She earned enough to buy herself a diamond ring and paid fifty dollars for a fur coat.

One bitter cold winter morning, she stood shivering on an icy downtown Dallas street corner waiting for the bus to take her to her house cleaning job. She heard her mind say, "Good as you can sew, good as you can sell Avon . . . , you ought to freeze to death."[46] Right then, she made a decision—she was going home. She told the woman standing with her, "I never intend to clean nobody's house in this town, or wherever, or nothing, as long as I live."[47]

She reactivated her Avon account and began selling products that netted her about three hundred dollars a month. Even though typical orders were three to eight dollars, she knew some of her customers could not afford them, so she cut out items and told the customer that the factory didn't have it. Sometimes, though, she "lost" the whole order only to find the person had money when they came for it. To add more income, she put a "Dressmaking" sign in her yard and began charging fifty cents to sew dresses.

By this time, she had married Leon Hunt. They had two daughters, Othella Ann and Leona Louise. By 1960 the Hunts were able to buy land and build their own house.

Through her three marriages, Annie Mae had four miscarriages and bore nine children, six of whom lived to adulthood. Grief over the loss of one of them drove her in the middle of the night to write a page-long poem, "Our Own Little Ruby Joyce."[48] The first verse says:

> *She were born into the world*
> *Those she never opened her eyes*
> *But we love her so much*
> *Our own daughter Little Ruby Joyce.*

When Othella was about two, Annie Mae got involved in politics. At that time, people paid a poll tax in order to vote. The amount was only $1.50, but the poll tax was intended to keep poor people, particularly African Americans, from voting. Annie Mae wrote out poll tax receipts for employers who wanted to register voters. Later, when voter registration became free, she had trouble convincing some people that the free registration was valuable.

From writing voter registration receipts, Annie Mae moved into more active help for Democratic candidates. She stuffed envelopes and licked stamps to mail candidate advertisements. She spoke at church. She expressed her opinions at her lodge, the Daughters of the Improved Benevolent Protective Order of Elks of the World. This organization came about after the all-white organization of Elks refused to admit African-American members. Those rejected organized their own Elks group, adding the word "Improved," and Annie Mae was a very active member of the women's division, earning her a service award for holding so many different offices. She was proud of the lodge's charity work and for many years attended annual meetings in distant cities.

She joined the Democratic Women of Dallas County and the Texas Black Caucus and used her membership to speak for candidates she wanted elected. She lobbied hard for the successful election of Ann Richards as state treasurer and later governor.

Annie Mae's efforts to get out voters became known to her Texas representative. Her highest ambition was to attend a Democratic presidential inauguration. She called her representative and told him she had money for tickets but didn't know how to get them. He sent a special courier to her house with tickets that admitted her to an inauguration party and provided her a seat in the parade viewing stands. Annie Mae rode the bus to Washington and at noon on a freezing cold January 20, 1977, watched Jimmy Carter sworn in as the thirty-ninth president of the United States.

As much as she enjoyed politics, she had a special place in her heart for the annual Homecoming held at the Good

Will Baptist Church in Washington County, Texas, the
country church where she grew up. She took her vacations
the last week in September each year so that she could
attend the event and spend the whole weekend visiting with
old friends.

As important as that church and the lodge and her
political work were, the thing she was most proud of was
her children. Four of them went to college. All of them had
good jobs. And by 1983 she could declare, "I'm broke out
with grandchildren."[49] When she died twenty years later,
she had sixty-nine descendants.

Before Annie Mae Hunt's death in October 2003,
Ruthe Winegarten edited her memoir, *I Am Annie Mae*.
In it Annie Mae recounted the happy as well as the tragic
events in her life. The musical of the same title showcasing
Annie Mae's strong personality was first staged in October
1987 and repeated several times later. It appeared in a six-
week run at Stages Theater in Houston, Texas, in 1989 and
twenty-seven years later at the Midtown Arts and Theater
Center Houston.

Annie Mae had been a staunch supporter of Congress-
woman Eddie Bernice Johnson from Johnson's earliest
career in politics. On October 28, 2003, Johnson entered
"Tribute to Annie Mae Hunt" into the Senate *Congressional
Record*.

Annie Mae had achieved her quest for dignity.

KING COTTON

The economy in the South before the Civil War was built on the production of cotton, a very labor-intensive crop. From preparation of the fields until the time the cotton left the plantation, it required a tremendous amount of work. Although many small farms worked with family labor, large plantations used slaves to produce the crop that provided income for the owner.

Two classes of slaves lived on a plantation—those who worked in the fields and those who worked in the plantation owner's home, most often called the Big House.

Field workers, in the first step of production, walked behind horse-drawn plows to create long furrows of over-turned soil. Then, cotton seeds were poked into the loosened dirt. When the plants began to grow, so did weeds, making it necessary to chop out the weeds with hoes to give the cotton plants room to grow.

Mature cotton plants produce beautiful flowers, but it is the white fibers found in the cotton bolls that are important. These fibers must be removed from the boll before they can be taken to the cotton gin where the seeds are removed, after which the cotton is sent to spinning mills to make the thread that is eventually woven into cloth.

Before the days of mechanical cotton pickers, the job of gathering cotton fibers was called "picking cotton" because a worker literally stooped over to pull fibers out of the many bolls on each plant. It was backbreaking work. Workers rarely straightened up as they pulled out the cotton and dropped it into the long sack they dragged along the rows.

Workers at the Big House had better food and better clothes, but they were no freer than the field slaves. Some cooked, others waited on the master's table. Some cleaned the large house. Some washed clothes, others sewed. They took care of the children. Sometimes a young slave was given to one of the master's children as a personal servant to do whatever its owner wished.

Slave quarters, built a little distance from the Big House, usually consisted of rows of small dwellings, often shanties. Slaves were allowed to marry—they called it "jumping over the broom" because that was part of the happy celebration. Still, no slave could leave the owner's property without per-mission, and those who did, carried a pass from the owner. If they left without permission, patrollers (called "paddy rollers" by the slaves) hunted them. When caught, they were cruelly whipped.

Slaves were valuable property. Some masters did not abuse their slaves simply because that was the owner's nature or perhaps because an injured slave could not work. But other owners had no regard for the welfare or comfort of some-thing they considered no more than a work animal. The slaves were simply property to be kept, sold, or given away.

President Lincoln abolished slavery when he issued the Emancipation Proclamation on January 1, 1863, but for most slaves freedom did not become reality until the end of the Civil War in 1865.

Most of the freed slaves had no money and consequently became sharecroppers. They still raised cotton on the owner's land but gave the owner part of the crop in return for living there. The landowner's part usually amounted to half.

Often sharecroppers were paid by tickets that usually could be redeemed only at a single store. At very large farms, workers had to buy what they needed from the company store and their tickets were redeemable only at that store. It was very common to have year-end accountings show that the renter owed more than his crop earned, causing perpetual debt.

When Annie Mae was picking cotton, most of it was grown in the eastern part of the state. Today, most of Texas cotton is grown in West Texas on massive farms, with machines taking the place of persons who once did the backbreaking work of cultivating and picking cotton.

MILDRED ELLA "BABE" DIDRIKSON ZAHARIAS (1911–1956)

PHOTOGRAPHY BY US OLYMPIC COMMITTEE, CRAWFORD FAMILY US OLYMPIC ARCHIVES

Mildred Ella "Babe" Didrikson Zaharias

1911–1956

B abe Zaharias was the best athlete in the world. If you didn't believe it, you could ask her, and she'd tell you that herself. And she was pretty much right. She was such a natural athlete that she outplayed the boys in the neighborhood where she grew up. Her high school coach wanted her as kicker for the football team but was overruled. She became a champion in eighty-meter hurdles, javelin throw, long jump, shotput, basketball, and golf. If it involved athletics, she set out to be the best. Today's top athletes dominate in one chosen field. Babe played many sports and excelled in all of them.

Mildred Ella Didriksen was born in Port Arthur, Texas, June 26, 1911. Her parents were Norwegian immigrants, Ole and Hannah Didriksen. Her father's work on an oil tanker brought him to Port Arthur, Texas. He was so fascinated with the area that he stayed, working on the Gulf coast from 1905 to 1908 to be able to bring his family to the United States.

Hannah arrived with three children, and soon after that four more were born. Mildred Ella was number six of seven children. Her mother always called her *Baden* (Baby) because she was the youngest girl, and this became "Babe." Another version of the story, possibly created by Babe, said that while playing sandlot baseball, she hit the ball farther than any of the boys, and they started calling her Babe after the most famous slugger of the day—Babe Ruth. The latter may not be the true version, but she did hit the ball farther than the boys she played with.

From an early age, Babe wanted to be the best, and usually was. She had a good model for creating stories about her exploits. Her father was a fabulous storyteller. His vivid accounts of his adventures on the high seas enthralled his children. Babe learned that a good yarn focuses attention on the speaker.

In Texas, though, Ole supported his family with woodworking skills learned from Babe's grandfather, who had been a cabinet-maker in Oslo, Norway. It was not steady work, however, and the income was often not enough. The family was poor and lived in a poor part of town.

Living on the hot, humid coast was very trying for Hannah. In Norway, her natural grace as an athlete gave her a reputation as a fine ice skater and skier, although she never entered competitions. Now her main task was to feed and raise her large family.

When Babe was about three, a hurricane damaged their home in Port Arthur so badly that they moved to

Beaumont, a little farther inland. Ole's jobs paid well when he had work, and Hannah took in laundry to supplement the income for their large brood. They were blue-collar, hardworking, frugal, and proud to be American. They observed both Norwegian and American holidays. The parents mixed English with Norwegian but switched to Norwegian when they wanted to speak privately. Religion didn't play much part in their lives, but there were lots of hugs and kisses for the children. The children knew they were loved. Sailor Ole had acquired very "salty" language, and the kids picked up that too.

All the kids had chores, but Babe preferred playing games. If she went missing, the family knew she would be somewhere in the neighborhood where a game was going on. When there was no game, she made the chore into one. If it was her turn to scrub the floor, she tied brushes on her feet and skated in the soap suds.

She was never still. In their working class neighborhood, kids played outside, and Babe was usually in the midst of the activity. She liked to roller skate. She was fast and strong. To her, winning was everything.

Her just-older sister Lillie was her constant companion. Babe was always dreaming up something new to do, sometimes dangerous things. She and Lillie tried jumping on and off boxcars of a slow-moving freight train. One of their practical jokes was to soap the trolley tracks so that the trolley slid to a stop, giving the other one time to jump on the back and disconnect the pole that supplied electricity to run the car. Then the conductor had to get out and reconnect it. One time Babe narrowly escaped being crushed when she slipped.

An exasperated Hannah didn't know what to do with this rambunctious child. Her patience ran thin when Babe returned home in a torn and dirty new dress Hannah had made. Babe ran when her mother started after her to punish her, but Hannah was hampered by a sprained ankle. Maybe it was Babe's sense of fairness, that she wasn't really a winner if the other person couldn't compete, but she stopped. Realizing her mother couldn't move fast, she said, "Mamma, don't run. I'll wait for you."[50] When Hannah hobbled up, she could only look down, laugh, and hug her worrisome child.

But one time, Babe crossed the line. She had been sent to the grocery store to bring home groceries. As she returned, she saw kids playing ball. She put the groceries down and joined the game. By the time her mother came looking for her, a dog was eating the last of the meat in the sack. This time Babe was marched home and into the bathroom where she received a proper licking. At that point Babe said she realized how much trouble she was causing her mother. From then on, she tried to make things easier for Hannah. Even after becoming famous, she looked out for her mother until Hannah's death.

Babe's athleticism was apparent by the second grade when she beat much older kids at the game of marbles. Her elementary school principal remembered being called outside to get Babe down from the top of the flagpole. She loved to have a good time, but she was not slow to use her mouth or her fists. When she didn't get what she wanted, she turned loose with some of her father's salty language. Many of the students, both girls and boys, were a little afraid of this wild, unpredictable creature.

By the time she was in junior high, she engaged exclusively in boys' sports. She never played with dolls as a little girl; hopscotch and jacks never appealed to her. She wanted action—foot races, baseball, football, jumping. She was so good at athletics that the principal let her play on the boys' teams.

At Beaumont High School her domination in sports continued. She won the YWCA swim match. She was on both the tennis and golf teams. Once, the halfback on the football team in a moment of braggadocio challenged her to a boxing match, telling her to hit him as hard as she could. She did, and her punch left him lying on the floor. She was not, however, built like an Amazon. She was thin and wiry, a beanpole of muscle, with hand/eye coordination that dazzled coaches.

Her high school basketball coach helped her learn the fundamentals of the game and hone her shooting skills. She knew she could kick farther than the kicker on the football team, and the coach was going to let her suit up and kick extra points, but the school administration would not give its approval.

Babe loved basketball, which had become a popular girls' sport several decades earlier. Before the 1880s it
was considered harmful for women to engage in active
sports. In the next three decades, things changed dramat-
ically as swimming and bicycling became acceptable. In
the 1890s basketball, volleyball, and field hockey became
part of the girls' physical education program. However,
when the Olympic Games were revived in 1896, women
were barred from the first two sports. By 1908 they were
allowed to compete in tennis, archery, and figure skating
and to participate in exhibitions of swimming, diving, and
gymnastics.

Besides pushing the boundaries of what was acceptable for girls to do, Babe rejected "girlie" things. She wore
no makeup, did not like frilly clothes, and had her hair
cropped short. Other girls considered her a rowdy tomboy
and didn't associate with her, but she was always the first to
be picked for physical sports, either boys' or girls', simply
because she was the best player. Shunned by the girls and
not really accepted by the boys, she didn't fit anywhere
in spite of the fact that classmates remembered her as
fun-loving.

Beaumont High School offered Home Economics,
a girls' course. And yet, Babe excelled there. The teacher
remembered her making a blue, long-sleeved dress, but
once it was graded, she promptly cut off the sleeves near
the shoulder because they got in her way. It seems incredible that rambunctious Babe would sit at a sewing machine

to construct a dress capable of winning First Place at a regional fair, but she did.

Somewhere along the way, an error changed the spelling of her last name to Didrikson, and she left it that way. She was not a particularly good student, but she passed all her courses. Winning was the goal she set early. In her autobiography, *The Life I've Led*, she said, "I knew exactly what I wanted to be when I grew up. My goal was to be the greatest athlete that ever lived."[51] The Olympics became her goal. She appointed Lillie as runner, and she would be the jumper and hurdler. She convinced neighbors to cut hedges lower between their house and the corner grocery store so she could practice, and she and Lillie began a fierce competition. Babe sailed over seven two-foot-wide hedges while Lillie raced down the street.

Money was tight for the Didriksons, just as it was for their neighbors. Shoes were a luxury for school. The family refused charity and instead skimped on food and made do with what they had. Ole even returned to the sea on occasions when there was no other work to do. In the musical family, there was not even enough money to buy Babe a harmonica she desperately wanted.

By the time she was thirteen Babe found a job sewing gunnysacks to hold potatoes. She was faster than anybody else, and, at a penny per completed sack, she earned sixty-eight cents an hour. All but a nickel went into Hannah's sugar bowl piggy bank. The family had very little, but they had each other, and even with all the exasperation she caused, home was her secure haven. And later, when she finally had her own money, Babe bought that harmonica and played it the rest of her life.

Her athleticism in high school caught the eye of Beaumont sportswriter "Tiny" Scurlock, and they formed a lifelong friendship. After reading Scurlock's articles touting the feats of Babe Didrikson, Melvin J. McCombs, the coach of the Employer's Casualty Insurance Company's women's semiprofessional basketball team, offered her the opportunity to play with them when she finished high school. She would earn three hundred dollars a month as a secretary and play on their team. The family needed money, and Babe talked the school into letting her leave early and return in the spring to take tests so she could get her diploma.

On February 17, 1930, eighteen-year-old Babe boarded the train for her new job in Dallas. She had $3.49 in her pocket, left over from money McCombs gave her for the ticket. Perhaps she had taken a high school typing course as she claimed or perhaps learned on the job. It mattered not—she was a Golden Cyclone, playing basketball and baseball and later competing in running, broad jump, eighty-meter hurdles, javelin, and shotput. Although she never liked swimming, she enjoyed fancy diving.

McCombs marveled at his luck but had his hands full. "Babe Didrikson was the easiest girl to coach and the hardest to handle of all athletes I have had in the past 15 years."[52] The team had several outstanding players, but Babe bragged about how she was going to be the best. Then she proceeded to do so, setting records that held for years.

Because she excelled in so many sports, McCombs entered her as a one-person team in the Amateur Athletic Union (AAU) meet. This competition in Evanston, Illinois, on July 16, 1932, qualified women athletes for the US team in the 1932 Olympics in Los Angeles two weeks later. At the end of three hours, Babe Didrikson held first place in broad jump, shotput, baseball throw, javelin throw, eighty-meter hurdles, and tied for high jump. Her personal score of thirty points was eight points more than the entire second place team. Babe was on her way to the Olympics.

She was twenty-one and still annoying teammates with hijinks on the train to Los Angeles. To anybody who would listen, she bragged that she was better than anybody else. She predicted she would come home with three gold medals. She did dominate the women's competition but at the expense of making friends.

Olympic rules at the time restricted women to three events. Babe's gold medals came as she predicted in the eighty-meter hurdles and the javelin throw. She tied for the high jump but was awarded second place because her method of going over the bar was declared illegal, although previous high jumps that way had not been questioned. It was certain that she would have won other gold medals had she been allowed to enter. As it was, sports headlines exploded, giving her fame as the "Greatest Woman Athlete of the World."[53]

She was a sportswriter's dream—unconventional enough to inspire good stories but such a superb athlete that nobody could argue with her success. Babe, however, was just warming up. Legendary sportswriter Grantland Rice thought she was clever and talented. He tried to think of something she couldn't do, so he asked about her sewing ability. She replied that she frequently made her clothes. Maybe so, but in her early days with the Golden Cyclones, she was so poor, other secretaries gave her dresses to wear. There is a picture of her working as a secretary in which it appears that her dress has been made smaller to fit her slim figure.

It was that slim, boyish figure, and close-cropped hair that caused hateful words from male sportswriters, but it was an unauthorized use of her photo to sell Dodge cars that caused the AAU to ban her for being a professional. She protested that she was not paid for the ad and that it had run without her permission, but she was barred from amateur competitions. She left the secretarial job.

As Olympic fame began to slip away, she was desperate to get back into the spotlight. She turned to stage shows. She strolled down the aisle in hat and heels, then took the stage and threw aside her coat to reveal a spangled uniform. Changing to track shoes, she raced on a treadmill, leaped hurdles, and hit imitation golf balls. Then she pulled out her harmonica. But a week of four or five shows a day was enough. She did not want to make money that way.

Since she was banned from amateur competition, she took part in exhibition games against or as part of men's teams, one of them a donkey basketball team. The money was good, and she sent most of it home to her family. But these exhibitions left an image of her as something of a freak that was hard to shake later.

She hadn't played golf since high school, but it was respectable, a game played by the wealthy. She was relentless in working to improve her game. She wrangled free lessons and benefited immensely from her 1935 tour with golf great Gene Sarazen. She clowned for the galleries, honed her skills, and best of all, she was back in the spotlight.

For all of her joking, she was serious about winning. She entered the Texas State Women's Golf championships where her opponents were wealthy, trained golfers. She played a grueling final match with the best of them and won. The victory was bittersweet—the US Golf Association promptly labeled Babe a professional and banned her from any more amateur golf tournaments.

Bertha Bowen, who was heavily involved in women's golf in Texas, was outraged that Babe would be treated poorly simply because she lacked clothes and polished manners. Bertha and her husband supported Babe. Bertha provided better clothes and got Babe to style her hair and tone down the rowdiness. Then she used her influence to change the Fort Worth Invitational golf tournament to the Women's Texas Open (now known as Texas Women's Open) so that both amateur and professional golfers could play. At times, though, the old Babe flared up. The association required women to wear girdles. Bertha coaxed her into one, but after one round in the girdle, Babe stormed back to the Bowen house and ripped it off with a few choice words, never to wear it again while playing.

In January 1938 Babe entered the men's Los Angeles Open. She needed money, and no rule said a woman couldn't play in the competition. She saw it as an opportunity to establish herself as the greatest woman golfer. She was paired with a Presbyterian minister and a professional wrestler named George Zaharias who had entered on a dare.

George, the son of Greek immigrants, knew what it was to be poor and to find success in sports. Wrestling was a show, something like a vaudeville performance by superb athletes. George knew how to play to the crowd paying money to hiss at his villainous scowling persona. Friends knew him as boisterous and fun-loving. Similar in background and in their search for the limelight, Babe and George felt an instant attraction. They started clowning around on the golf course and provided sportswriters colorful copy for their papers. The two athletes each claimed it was love at first sight.

They were married January 3, 1938, at the home of a wrestling promoter in St. Louis, on a weekend when appearances allowed them to be in the same place. The honeymoon came in April a year later. They flew to Hawaii, then went on to Australia where George, who by this time was acting as Babe's manager, had booked her to play exhibitions.

Babe wanted to return to amateur sports, but the US Golf Association rules required her to sit out three years.

Unable to stay out of sports, she took up tennis. She characteristically sought out good coaches and practiced relentlessly. Just when she was ready for tournaments, she found out that her golf professional status carried over to tennis and interfered with her return to amateur sports. She dropped tennis and turned to bowling. She still kept up golf exhibitions, many with famous entertainers like Bob Hope and Bing Crosby. Hope quipped, "There's only one thing wrong about Babe and myself. I hit the ball like a girl and she hits it like a man."[54]

During World War II she played tournaments for armed service charities, keeping in the limelight with personalities such as Babe Ruth. She and George had a home in Denver, Colorado, and she taught kids in detention homes and orphanages how to swim, golf, and play ball.

By 1945 she was again able to play in amateur golf tournaments. She was in Indianapolis ready for the semifinals in the Western Women's Open when she got a call from George saying her mother had had a heart attack. Hannah had always been Babe's biggest supporter. Babe was frantic to get home, but George and her sister told her to keep competing. It was what Hannah would want.

Hannah died the night Babe won the semifinals. There was no seat on any transportation to get home. Devastated, Babe sat in her room with friends, playing her harmonica, saying nothing. She won the tournament the next day. The tortuous trip home stretched to two days as she was bumped off flights by priority passengers.

For the next nine years, Babe Zaharias dominated women's golf. She won the US Women's Amateur in 1946, and the British Ladies' Amateur the following year. At this point Babe turned professional. There was no organization for women professional golfers, so she and five others established the Ladies Professional Golf Association (LPGA) in 1948. She was the leading money winner on the LPGA circuit from 1948 to 1951. She won the US Women's Open in 1948 and repeated her victory in 1950 and 1954, this last time after cancer surgery.

Severe pain had sent her to the hospital for tests in 1953. She had surgery for colon cancer but was determined to play again. She joined President and Mrs. Eisenhower to inaugurate the 1954 Cancer Crusade and then proceeded to win five tournaments.

But a victory over cancer was not to be. She was only forty-five when she died on September 27, 1956, in Galveston's John Sealy Hospital. George and a young golfer named Betty Dodd had been at her side during her last struggle.

The Associated Press named the irrepressible, multitalented sports woman as the Greatest Female Athlete of the first half of the twentieth century. In the *SportsCentury* list of the top North American athletes of the twentieth century, only ten men are listed above her, and none of them come near to matching Babe Didrikson Zaharias's domination in so many sports.

THE OLYMPIC GAMES, ANCIENT AND MODERN

The ancient Olympic Games, honoring the Greek god Zeus, were held at Olympia in southwest Greece. The first recorded winner in 776 BCE was a cook named Koroibus who ran a single race on a straight track one *stade* long. (A *stade*, source of our word *stadium*, is 192 meters or about two hundred yards.) Other events were added later—longer footraces, weightlifting, javelin and discus throws, the long jump, and a no-holds-barred boxing/wrestling match. Chariot races took place a little distance away. Winners received a crown of laurel leaves. These competitions began to decline after Rome conquered Greece. Near the end, Emperor Nero declared himself the winner of the chariot race even after falling out of his chariot. The games ceased in 393 CE when they were banned as pagan.

In the aftermath of earthquakes and floods, the original site was buried. Discovered in 1766, it yielded fourteen thousand objects that were placed in a museum there. Today, visitors walk among the ruins at Olympia and dig their toes in the twenty-five-centuries-old marble starting block on the original course.

The Modern Olympics revived the games in 1896. Frenchman Pierre de Coubertin dreamed of international amateur sports competition as a way to create better understanding between nations. The five rings of the Olympic logo represent Africa, Asia, America, Europe, and Oceana, in the colors of national flags.

The marathon was a new event for 1896. Runners covered nearly twenty-five miles, the distance of the legendary run that carried news from the plain of Marathon to Athens of the Greek victory over Persian invaders. The next year, Boston, Massachusetts, held a marathon that has been repeated every year since 1897. The 1908 London Games increased the distance to twenty-six and two-tenths miles (42.195 kilometers), the distance from Windsor Castle to the royal box in the stadium, and that distance was made official in 1921.

Winter games began in 1924, and in 1994, summer and winter games began alternating every two years. The Olympic flame, ignited by the sun's rays at Olympia, is carried to the site of the games to signify the start. It is extinguished at the end and reignited four years later for the next Olympic Games.

Claudia Alta "Lady Bird" Taylor Johnson

1912–2007

"**P**urty as a lady bird."[55] These words are the oft-quoted source of the nickname for little Claudia Taylor, ascribed to her African-American nurse Alice Tittle. According to Lady Bird herself, her childhood playmates, the children of the woman who did their wash, gave her that name. Regardless of the source, the nickname stuck. Few people remember her given name, the one her mother chose to honor her brother Claude Pattillo, but the association of beauty with Lady Bird Johnson is more than nickname deep. As wife of the president of the United States, she worked to make the nation conscious of the beauty of nature.

Claudia Taylor was born in Karnack, Texas, December 22, 1912. Her mother, Minnie Lee Pattillo Taylor, had grown up the privileged daughter of a wealthy family in central Alabama. Her father, Thomas Jefferson Taylor Jr., was from the same county but worlds away from Pattillo wealth. He fell in love with Minnie after seeing her flying through the countryside on a horse. When Minnie's father objected to his daughter marrying someone he considered socially inferior, Taylor vowed to become wealthier than his father-in-law. And he fulfilled that vow.

On a whim, Taylor moved to Karnack, a tiny farm and timber community of four hundred people in East Texas near Caddo Lake. It had no paved streets. He bought property in town and opened a store blazoned with the sign "T.J. Taylor, Dealer in Everything."[56] Cotton was the area's cash crop, and the budding entrepreneur bought a cotton gin, an operation that separated seeds from cotton fibers so the cotton could be processed into cloth.

Feeling sufficiently established, he went back to Alabama to marry Minnie, but her parents were no more receptive than they had been the first time. Minnie, perhaps in an act of defiance, married Taylor anyway. Her family refused to attend the ceremony.

Returning to Karnack, the newlyweds lived in a house Taylor had built next to the store so that he could work around the clock. Minnie, isolated from the comforts she had known, found solace in the crates of books she had brought with her. And she kept ordering more. She loved the classics and Lady Bird remembered her mother reading Greek myths to her.

CLAUDIA ALTA "LADY BIRD" TAYLOR JOHNSON
(1912–2007)
LBJ LIBRARY PHOTO BY UNKNOWN

With much love,

Minnie had no interest in being a traditional house-wife. With little else to do in the tiny community, she bought a huge Hudson automobile and hired a chauffeur to drive her around the countryside where roads were so bad that they sometimes got stuck. Locals viewed Minnie Taylor as eccentric, riding in her chauffeured car wearing a cap or scarf on her head and keeping a veil over her face. It is likely that she was subject to migraine headaches, and the veil would have filtered light that is painful to migraine sufferers. Lady Bird had shadowy memories of her mother being sick and losing some of her hair and wearing something on her head much of the time.

Once a year Minnie escaped with her sister Effie Pattillo to New York or Chicago where they enjoyed the opera. She continually added to her huge collection of recorded albums. In an era when women still could not vote, she campaigned in elections, perhaps to annoy her husband because they often were on different sides of an issue.

After the birth of two sons, Minnie returned to Alabama with the boys for an extended period of time. Thinking to please his wife, Taylor bought a two-story, seventeen-room antebellum mansion made of bricks fashioned by slave labor. Not long after that, Lady Bird was born in the Brick House.

Lady Bird was never around her brothers very much. Tommy and Tony, who were eight and ten years older than she, were shipped off to boarding school in the New York

Catskills. During the summer they attended camps in New Mexico.

During her earliest years her playmates were children of the hired help. Being alone so much, she found her own amusement. "I would quite naturally explore the woods and climb trees and do all sorts of things that you might speak of as tomboy things."[57]

Wandering in the rural area, she encountered Spanish moss hanging from cypress trees among the bayous and wildflowers blanketing the fields. In the springtime the Brick House swam in a sea of yellow jonquils. Magnolia trees bore enormous white blossoms and crepe myrtle bushes of various colors burst into bloom. White dogwood dotted the forest, and redbud branches sported a coating of color before putting out leaves. She soaked up this natural beauty. As an adult, it was her passion to preserve it.

Lady Bird lost her mother before she was six. Minnie Taylor fell down the stairs at the Brick House and was taken to the hospital in Marshall where she died. Because it was cotton-picking season, the busiest time for Taylor's business, he kept working. The only reaction Lady Bird saw to her mother's death was his angry response to the minister who tried to console the family. She learned at that point to keep her emotions to herself. As an adult she became quiet and still, seemingly zoned out, when a situation became unpleasant.

After her mother's death, Lady Bird's father took her to the store with him while he worked. As he hunched over his ledgers, Lady Bird wandered among the items he sold. Because he worked late, he set up a bed for her without considering the coffins stacked nearby. When Lady Bird asked what the long boxes were for, he thought a minute then replied, "Dry goods, honey."[58] He did not want to frighten her because there was much local superstition about ghosts. The Brick House itself was said to have its own resident ghost of a young woman who died there.

A few months later he sent her to her grandfather in Alabama. He put her on the train alone with a sign around her neck saying "Deliver this child to John Will Pattillo."[59] When she returned to Karnack, her Aunt Effie came with her. Minnie's unmarried sister had no home of her own but visited among relatives. She had been a talented pianist and a painter, but she frequently suffered from various unnamed ailments. Effie loved Lady Bird and came to take care of her, but before many years, Lady Bird was the one taking care of Effie with her real or imagined illnesses.

Effie introduced her niece to new things. The whole Pattillo family believed in diet and physical exercises espoused by Dr. John Kellogg, the inventor of the cereal that bears his name. They routinely visited his sanatorium in Battle Creek, Michigan, and when Lady Bird was eleven, Effie took her there. The sight of elderly Dr. Kellogg furiously peddling his bicycle around the property and leading vigorous calisthenics amused the young girl. Dr. Kellogg preached exercise and eating vegetables. Dinner each evening had an unfamiliar formality for the young girl who had never eaten on a starched linen tablecloth set with china and fingerbowls. As the only young person there, Lady Bird received lots of attention.

Taylor remained buried in his work. He now owned a second gin. Eli Whitney's invention of the modern cotton gin speeded up the tedious process of removing seeds from the cotton, making cotton a profitable crop.

East Texas, like most of the South, had favorable conditions for the crop. Many descendants of former slaves remained in the area where their parents had lived. While a few might own their small farms, both whites and African Americans who did not own land were often sharecroppers living on the property of large landowners. As rent, they paid the owner a part of their crop, usually half.

Taylor had continued to buy land and had many sharecroppers. They bought everything they needed from his store that literally sold "Everything"—food, seed, plows, furniture, even coffins. At the end of cotton season, tenants' store purchases were charged against their portion of the cotton proceeds. In years of drought or when rain ruined the cotton, the value would likely not be enough to cover what they owed Taylor. Even when there was enough to cover current charges, it might not erase debt from earlier years. Some of the land Taylor acquired had been deeded to him as payment for store debts. Eventually "Mr. Boss" owned fifteen thousand acres. He was the largest landowner in the county.

Lady Bird was aware that her family had more money than others in the community, but she still attended the tiny local school whose sessions were regulated by the need for children to help their parents at planting and harvest time. But for high school, she had to go elsewhere.

After her summer at the Kellogg sanatorium, Lady Bird enrolled in school at Jefferson, about fifteen miles away. Fifty years earlier, Jefferson had been the second largest town in Texas. Ships navigated the bayou from the Red River, bringing goods from New Orleans and points farther away. Wealthy citizens built beautiful homes, but the town declined when the railroad went to nearby Marshall. Jefferson officials had spurned railroad baron Jay Gould's offer to bring his railroad through Jefferson, and an angry Gould predicted the town's demise. Today, Jefferson's frozen-in-time atmosphere remains a tourist attraction, and guests can read Gould's prediction of Jefferson's doom in the Excelsior House Hotel register.

Lady Bird's brother Tony lived in Jefferson, but she and Effie did not stay with him. Instead, they boarded with the two elderly, well-educated Emmett sisters. Effie reveled in having companions who shared her love of culture, and Lady Bird finally had friends her own age.

In Jefferson she also had her first encounter with a bicycle since Karnack had no paved streets to ride on. "I managed to stay on, but I discovered myself going downhill and I didn't know how to stop, much less slow up. I finally headed straight for a mailbox on the side of the road and did indeed stop with a loud crescendo and got tossed over the bars and into the ditch. Not much damage except a little bruised and scratched."[60]

Returning home for her last two years of high school, she attended Marshall High School about twenty-five miles away. One of her father's employees drove her there each day, but she made him stop three blocks away from the school because the truck smelled of hides. Finally her father bought her a car. She got a license, and the fifteen-year-old senior drove herself.

For all of her father's wealth, she remained painfully shy. As graduation neared, she feared she might have to make the traditional valedictorian speech by the top student, and being salutatorian, second best student, held the same terror. She deliberately allowed her grades to slip so that her best friend Emma could be valedictorian. A girl one-half grade point below Emma became salutatorian. Lady Bird, a safe one full point below Emma, was spared the agony of making a commencement speech.

Against her father's wishes, she enrolled in St. Mary's College for Girls, a two-year school in Dallas. For the first time, she found ideas that stretched her mind and a wonderful English teacher who taught her the value of choosing the right words in writing. Sewing and cooking classes were disasters, but she enjoyed the anonymity of performing in plays.

In 1930 the Depression deepened, but she arrived at the University of Texas in Austin with her own car and a charge account at Neiman-Marcus. Fashionable clothes, however, held no interest. She did enjoy picnics with university friends but remained serious about her studies, particularly history, her major. She received high grades, all except in chemistry where friends helped her squeak through with a D.

Even with that one low grade, she still graduated with honors. She became interested in journalism and remained another year to get a degree in that, also with honors. Along the way she learned shorthand that served her well in recording conversations and events during the years she was in public life.

At twenty-one, she considered a career as a journalist, but less than three months after leaving the university, she met Lyndon Johnson. The lanky Texan intrigued her. He always seemed to be in a hurry. He asked her to marry him on the second date and ten weeks later, November 17, 1934, they were on their way to a honeymoon in Mexico after a ceremony in San Antonio. Like her mother before her, no one from her family was there. The groom forgot to buy a wedding ring, forcing the best man to run across the street to Sears before the ceremony and purchase a $2.50 ring. She wore it for years before getting an expensive ring.

Johnson earned a meager salary as legislative secretary to US congressman Richard Kleberg, a member of the wealthy family that owned the huge King Ranch in South Texas. Lady Bird was thrust into unfamiliar homemaking duties in a tiny Washington, DC apartment. Nonetheless, she served many guests her husband brought home to eat her southern cooking.

Having grown up watching her father handle his accounts, she took charge of household finances. Her good business sense proved valuable, especially since she was heir to part of her mother's estate. When Lyndon Johnson decided to run for the US House of Representatives in 1937, she financed his winning campaign with ten thousand dollars borrowed against that inheritance.

Knowing they needed to have a steady income, Lady Bird used inheritance money to buy a struggling Austin radio station. The call letters became KLBJ, and she took an active role in running the station. She actively managed LBJ Holdings, which grew to include an FM station and Austin's first TV station, KTBC-TV7, as well. The stations remained Johnson family business for years.

In 1941 a US Senate seat became vacant, and Lyndon Johnson set his sights on it. Lady Bird worked to overcome her shyness to help her husband campaign, but he did not win. However he kept his seat as congressman. When Pearl Harbor was bombed that December, Lyndon Johnson was the first member of Congress to join the armed forces. During the months he was in service she ran his office, learning the inner workings of politics that were useful for the rest of their long service in Washington.

During Johnson's twelve years in the House of Representatives, daughter Lynda Bird Johnson was born in 1944 and Luci Baines Johnson three years later. Their father joked about the advantage of having the same LBJ initials for all of their luggage.

Seven years after losing his first bid for a Senate seat, Johnson tried again. In this era the person chosen as Democratic candidate in the Texas primary was a sure winner. Lady Bird traveled the state to gather votes for her husband, even brushing off a car accident in which her car turned over. Her husband's narrow victory margin of eighty-seven votes in the primary caused detractors to dub him "Landslide Lyndon," but he easily defeated the Republican candidate at election time and returned to Washington as the junior senator from Texas. He served from 1949 to 1961.

During the years her husband was making the long climb from freshman senator to majority leader, Lady Bird was at his side. To him, she was always "Bird," and he depended on her counsel. She often had to soothe hard feelings caused by her husband's harsh words to co-workers. She studied public speaking and began to pay more attention to her clothes. After he bought the ranch near Johnson City, Texas, where he grew up, she supervised the restoration of the old farmhouse. It would later become the Texas White House, now part of the Lyndon B. Johnson National Historical Park.

At the 1960 Democratic convention, the Johnsons were disappointed when he was not chosen as the nominee for the presidency. But John F. Kennedy invited Lyndon Johnson to be his running mate since he would appeal to southern voters. Again, Lady Bird Johnson, now more confident, took an active part in the campaign. When the Kennedy-Johnson ticket won, she assumed added duties as wife of the vice president of the United States.

Three years later as re-election loomed, the Johnsons went to Dallas with the Kennedys. They were riding in the second car behind President and Mrs. Kennedy when shots rang out, killing President Kennedy. That afternoon aboard the president's plane, Lyndon Baines Johnson was sworn in as thirty-sixth president of the United States. Lady Bird Johnson was suddenly first lady.

While the nation mourned with glamorous young widow Jackie Kennedy, sedate Lady Bird Johnson began recording her daily experiences. "I began talking my White House diary into a tape recorder at our home, The Elms, two or three days after November 22, 1963. A little of it was recorded in hotel rooms on our trips, and in my bedroom at the LBJ Ranch, but the great bulk of it was done in a small room in the southwest corner of the second floor of the White House . . . I love that room."[61] The transcribed tapes became *Lady Bird Johnson: A White House Diary*, published in 1970.

As president, Johnson used his political skills to gain passage of the Civil Rights Act of 1964 outlawing segregation and discrimination. Lady Bird followed her passion to beautify Washington, starting with the White House garden. Her efforts spread through the capital and finally across America as she fought to remove unsightly billboards and urged the seeding of wildflowers common to each state.

Within weeks of taking office, the Johnsons had to focus on the 1964 election. Lady Bird, now a confident public speaker, set out to gather votes on her own. She became the first presidential wife to campaign solo by making a four-day, eight-state whistlestop campaign through the South, greeting crowds from the rear platform of the vintage train known as The Lady Bird Special.

Lyndon Johnson won by a large majority. Because he had grown up knowing the pinch of poverty, he launched his "Great Society" programs to improve lives of poor people. He orchestrated sixty education bills, supplied federal support of the arts and humanities, and got Congress to pass the 1965 Medicare Amendment to Social Security so older citizens could get medical care. The Voting Rights Act of the same year outlawed poll taxes aimed at keeping people of color from voting. Three years later another Civil Rights Act banned discrimination in selling and renting property. Lady Bird, his close advisor, participated in discussions on the issues.

But dark days came. In spite of efforts to develop economically depressed regions, riots rocked sections of American cities. As the death rate continued to rise in the unpopular Vietnam conflict, outrage followed. Lady Bird felt every criticism aimed at her husband. On August 10, 1967, she recorded, "Today's poll has Lyndon down to thirty-nine percent—the lowest he has ever been. My instinct tells me the only reaction to it should be to work harder, be staunch, and keep smiling. But it is hard."[62]

There had been happy moments, of course, during their time in the White House—the marriage of both daughters, the birth of a grandson and a granddaughter. Lady Bird was proud of the Clean Air Act and the Highway Beautification Act, the protection of wilderness spaces and unspoiled seashores she had championed.

But the ugly mood in America made it clear that Lyndon Johnson had little chance of winning re-election. Using words Lady Bird provided as the final statement in his speech, Lyndon Johnson surprised everyone by saying he would not accept his party's nomination for another term.

On January 20, 1969, they observed Richard Nixon's inauguration, then flew home to their Texas ranch where five hundred longtime friends welcomed them. At last they were home. "We went into the house then. The fire was burning on the raised hearth in the living room, flickering on the familiar pictures and old books and the big comfortable chairs."[63] The ranch fifty miles west of Austin that she had seeded with wildflowers truly was home to them.

Plans went forward to build the LBJ Presidential Library at the University of Texas in Austin, and Lady Bird was appointed a trustee of the university. She continued to manage LBJ Holdings. For four years they enjoyed the ranch before Lyndon Johnson's fatal heart attack on January 22, 1973.

At sixty-one, Lady Bird remained active in running the family business. She enjoyed her seven grandchildren, even going whitewater rafting with her grandson. She raised money to build a hiking/biking trail along the Colorado River in Austin. For her seventieth birthday, she gave land at the edge of Austin for a Wildflower Research Center to promote the use of natural plants and wildflowers. It was renamed for her on her eighty-fifth birthday.

Although the Johnsons had deeded the ranch to the United States as a historic site in 1972, she retained the right to stay there as long as she lived. She was ninety-four when she died on July 11, 2007. Lady Bird is buried beside her husband under huge live oak trees in the Johnson Family Cemetery at the ranch in Stonewall, Texas, where wildflowers abound.

FIRST LADIES

First Lady is the designation Americans give to the wife of the president of the United States. The first time the phrase was used is said to have been at Dolley Madison's funeral. Before that, the president's wife was sometimes referred to as "Mrs. Presidentress."

The role of first lady for the most part has been to supervise the White House, to entertain world dignitaries, and to attend functions with the president. However, not every first lady was the president's wife. James Buchanan and Grover Cleveland were not married when they were elected. Buchanan's niece Harriet Lane and Cleveland's sister Rose Cleveland served as their hostesses.

For the four widowed presidents, it was Thomas Jefferson's daughter Martha Randolph, Andrew Jackson's niece Emily Donelson, Martin Van Buren's daughter-in-law Angelica Van Buren, and Chester A. Arthur's sister Mary McElroy who acted as hostesses.

First ladies had other responsibilities besides hosting White House dinners. Lady Bird Johnson and Michelle Obama had previously held executive positions. Hillary Clinton became a politician herself, first as senator from New York and later as a presidential candidate.

Many were ardent supporters of social change. John Quincy Adams's wife Louisa urged her husband to take up women's rights during his years as congressman following his presidency. Woodrow Wilson's first wife, Ellen, lived long enough to know that Congress had passed a bill to improve Washington housing for poor African Americans and immigrants. Wilson's second wife Edith took such control of her husband's duties after his debilitating stroke that some felt she had assumed his office.

Eleanor Roosevelt advocated civil rights and the rights of women and was a leader in the formation of the United Nations. Jacqueline Kennedy supervised the restoration and redecoration of the White House. Betty Ford was a strong advocate for women's health and the Equal Rights Amendment. For Rosalynn Carter the issue was mental health, and she and her husband Jimmy Carter actively participated in Habitat for Humanity building projects after he left office.

Nancy Reagan took an active role in the fight against drug and alcohol abuse with her "Just Say No" campaign. Former librarian Laura Bush and her mother-in-law Barbara Bush promoted literacy. Michelle Obama pushed healthy eating habits for children and aid for military families. For Lady Bird Johnson, though, it was making the environment a place of beauty.

Clotilde Pérez García

1917–2003

Clotilde Pérez García was proud of her Hispanic roots and promoted pride in Hispanic heritage by founding genealogical association to enable descendants to trace their ancestry. She translated Mexican historical accounts and wrote books about Spanish South Texas. For her efforts, she received honors from King Carlos of Spain. A physician, she devoted herself to the care of the poor in Corpus Christi, Texas. During her forty years as a medical doctor, she delivered about ten thousand babies and was awed each time "holding each individual, a precious, new person."[64] She worked diligently in the area of civil rights concerning Mexican Americans and marched with protestors. She was a teacher who promoted education, serving on the board of regents for Del Mar College and donating her library and personal papers to Texas A&M University–Corpus Christi. Through her lengthy public service, she became known as the legendary Dr. Cleo.

Clotilde P. García was born on January 11, 1917, in Cuidad Victoria, Tamaulipas, Mexico, about two hundred miles southwest of Brownsville, Texas. She was the second daughter and fourth child of José García García and Faustina Pérez de García. Two younger brothers and another sister would complete the family after they came to Texas.

Clotilde's parents were from an area of Tamaulipas colonized by José de Escandón, sometimes called "father" of the lower Rio Grande Valley.[65] The king of Spain granted Escandón the right to establish missions and towns in the area between Tampico and the San Antonio River. This whole area was later known as Nuevo Santander. This gave rise to Mexico's claim to land north of the Rio Grande following the Texas Revolution.

Escandón became governor of Nuevo Santander in 1748. He then granted other individuals the right to establish towns. These included Camargo, Reynosa, and Meir in Mexico. In 1755 he granted Tomás Sánchez de la Barrera y Garza permission to found Laredo, the largest and most successful permanent Spanish settlement in lower southwest Texas. At that time San Antonio, the other permanent Texas settlement, had been settled thirty-five years earlier by four hundred families from the Canary Islands.

Both of Clotilde's parents graduated from the normal (teachers') school in Ciudad Victoria and were trained educators. The couple stressed the importance of education to their children. José García was a strong father figure to his growing family and taught in various schools to support the family. He had a great love of history and was a friend of historian Carlos E. Castañeda. Both men were from Camargo, Tamaulipas, Mexico. Castañeda came to Texas several

CLOTILDE PÉREZ GARCÍA (1917–2003)

years before the Garcías and eventually became an eminent scholar and historian of the Spanish Southwest during his professorship at the University of Texas in Austin.

Clotilde's mother Faustina was a loving person with a nurturing personality, encouraging her children to be the best they could be. As Catholics, the couple raised their children in the church. The children were held to high standards of conduct and expected to become useful citizens. But times were chaotic in Mexico.

Prior to Mexico's 1910 Revolution, the government had been in the hands of dictatorial president Porfirio Días for nearly thirty-five years. When revolt finally came, it led to a decade of turmoil with frequent turnover of presidents. In this chaotic era, Pancho Villa became a folk hero, loved by the poor and a thorn in the side of Mexican officials. Raids across the border into US territory sent the US Army on a futile search for the bandit.

During this decade of violent government overthrows, middle-class, educated Mexicans like the Garcías had little voice. They were caught in the conflict between opposing forces struggling to gain control of the Mexican government. This lack of stability prompted the Garcías to move their family legally to the United States when Clotilde was just three months old.

They settled in Mercedes, Texas, just five miles north of the Rio Grande about forty miles west of Brownsville. This area, known as the Valley, has warm winters making it a mecca for people referred to as snowbirds to escape cold winters. Enthusiasts also come to observe bird and butterfly migrations.

The soil and weather make the Valley a prime location for growing crops, particularly citrus fruit. Not a valley at all, the floodplain of the Rio Grande produces much of the grapefruit grown in the United States. Ruby Red grapefruit, the result of a natural occurrence in an orchard in 1929, is state fruit. Its popularity forced out the cultivation of white grapefruit.

Grapefruit cultivation had just begun when the Garcías arrived in the Valley to join extended family members who were farmers and merchants. Since they were not farmers and Clotilde's father had no certification to teach in the United States, José and Faustina García opened a dry goods store in Mercedes.

The Garcías continued to stress the value of education and made sure the children focused on their studies. They were expected to choose a professional career, with medicine being particularly favored. Six of the seven García children became doctors. José García used his wide-ranging knowledge of subjects from Aztec civilization to mathematics and literature to mentor his children at home and supplement their schoolwork.

Clotilde spent a happy childhood attending public school where she studied hard, engaging in afterschool baseball games, and studying music and art. When she was a little older, she helped her parents in the store when she had free time. After graduating from Mercedes High

School in 1934, she entered nearby Edinburg Junior College and two years later received an associate of arts degree, which qualified her to teach.

From junior college, she went directly to the University of Texas at Austin where she chose a pre-med course with a major in zoology and a minor in chemistry. While there, she had the pleasure of meeting her father's friend Professor Castañeda. After receiving her bachelor of arts degree in 1938, she expected to follow in the footsteps of her two older brothers, José Antonio (J.A.) and Héctor García, and study medicine, but plans to enter medical school had to be put on hold.

The Great Depression was in full swing. The shattered economy had stripped away jobs and money was scarce. Small businesses like the Garcías' dry goods store were hit hard because their customers could not afford to buy merchandise or services. Since Clotilde was qualified to teach, she turned to that to bring the family extra income. For the next twelve years she taught in the South Texas communities of Benavides, Hebbronville, and Mercedes. She found it very satisfying to get to know the people in the towns where she worked.

At twenty-three, Clotilde got her American citizenship. In 1943 she married Hipólito Canales, who was from Hebbronville. Their son, José Antonio (Tony) Canales, was born in Brownsville, Texas, the next year. The marriage however did not last. She reared Tony with the same emphasis on education and expectation of a professional career that she had received from her parents. He finished high school and enrolled at the University of Texas where he earned a bachelor's degree, but differed from his mother, aunt, and uncles in that he chose the legal field instead of medicine. He received a Doctorate of Law from St. Mary's University of San Antonio in 1969 and was admitted to the bar that same year. Subsequently, he was named one of the Best Lawyers in America and admitted to practice before the US Supreme Court.

Clotilde García's own path led her to return to the University of Texas in 1950 to earn a master of education degree. Her thesis centered on Latin American literature and reflected her interest in her Hispanic heritage.

In spite of her pleasure in teaching, her family encouraged her to return to the pursuit of a career as a physician. Almost as soon as she finished her advanced education degree, she entered the University of Texas School of Medicine in Galveston (UTMB) where her older brothers had studied. But she faced two obstacles—she was a woman in a male-dominated field and she was a Mexican American. Six other women in her class faced the gender problem, but she was the only Hispanic. Clotilde's forceful personality and determination carried her through.

Her MD was granted in 1954, and she moved to Corpus Christi, where she completed her residency at Corpus Christi Memorial Hospital the following year. Since her older brothers had already established their medical practices there, she opened her own private practice, one of the first Mexican-American women to practice medicine in Texas.

As a general practitioner, she made it her goal to care for all people, especially the poor, who were almost always Mexican Americans. Besides treating ailments, she also educated her patients on infant care, nutrition, and how to live healthier lives. She worked many hours caring for the long line of patients who came to her office, seeing them on a first-come, first-served basis. She developed a personal relationship with them and was deeply concerned about each individual. When a patient died, she often attended the funeral to offer consolation to the grieving family. To her patients, she was a caring friend. She was Dr. Cleo.

Obstetrics was a major part of her practice. She estimated she had brought something like ten thousand babies into the world. She was a confirmed Democrat, supporting the elections of presidents John F. Kennedy and Lyndon B. Johnson on the national level, as well as Texas governor Ann Richards. She often laughed when she delivered a baby that she had "just delivered another Democrat."[66] But she was especially proud to be present at the birth of all three of her grandchildren, to whom she became a devoted grandmother.

Although no longer a teacher, she maintained a keen interest in education. Dr. Cleo founded the Carmelite Day Nursery Parents and Friends Club to provide support for the work of nurturing and teaching small children. At the other end of the school age range, she served for twenty-two years as a regent for Del Mar College in Corpus Christi. This community college prepares students for pursuit of bachelor degrees and also offers training for students entering trades. In gratitude for her efforts to support the college, the college named its Science and Health Building in her honor.

She was national health director for the League of United Latin American Citizens (LULAC) during the 1960s and also took part in evaluating Medicaid in Texas. Knowing that jobs would provide money for better food and living conditions, she focused on employment in addition to health issues. She spent a year on the national board of directors of SER (Service, Employment, Redevelopment) Jobs for Progress. She served three years on the board of directors for the Nueces County Antipoverty Program in the early 1970s.

Because of her own heritage, she was particularly interested in making sure that people understood the important contribution of Hispanics to our country. In the 1970s she began to do serious historical research on South Texas and northern Mexico. She was a member of the Nueces County Historical Society and the Nueces County Historical Commission, and was appointed to the Texas Historical Commission. During America's Bicentennial, she served on the American Revolution Bicentennial Commission. She wanted Hispanics to be proud of their heritage.

This interest led to her first book, a translation of *The Siege of Camargo*, the account of an 1812 Indian uprising.

She followed this with eight more publications, one of them about Blas María de la Garza Falcón who founded Camargo under a grant from José de Escandón. Other books focused on Padre José Nicolás Ballí, the priest for whom Padre Island is named, and Alonso Álvarez de Pineda, the commander of a fleet who created the first map of the Gulf of Mexico coastline.

Dr. Cleo's interest in her own ancestry led her to make resources available for others to do genealogical research about their families. She donated books and microfilm to the Corpus Christi Public Library to help Hispanics trace their ancestry. She and her sister Dr. Dalia P. García were among the group of interested persons who founded the Spanish American Genealogical Association (SAGA) in 1987. She led the organization through its first five years, and supported SAGA's activities. One important accomplishment was the donation of funds to purchase hundreds of rolls of microfilm focusing on early settlers in South Texas, especially in the area south of the Nueces River in the Brownsville–Corpus Christi–Laredo triangle.

The work she had done to promote awareness of the Hispanic past reached the attention of King Juan Carlos I of Spain. In 1990, he awarded Clotilde García the Royal American Order of Isabella the Catholic. She traveled to the Spanish Embassy in Washington, DC for presentation of the medal.

She took up causes supported by her brother Dr. Héctor García. After he returned from serving in Italy in World

War II, he began investigating conditions among migrant workers where disease and malnourishment were rampant. He was also concerned with Mexican-American veterans. The quest for fair treatment of Mexican-American veterans and the need to combat discrimination led to the founding of the American G.I. Forum in 1948.

A year after its formation, the Forum became involved in the controversy surrounding the burial of Army private Felix Longoria. He had been killed in the Philippines in 1945, and when his body was returned in 1949, his widow Beatriz Longoria asked to hold the funeral at the funeral home. The funeral director told her that he could not do that because his other customers would not want a funeral for a Mexican American at the place they held their funerals. He offered to hold the service at the widow's home in the segregated part of town. National broadcasts carried the news of the veteran who gave his life for his country but was denied a common courtesy afforded to white soldiers. Dr. Héctor García led the G.I. Forum to petition Senator Lyndon B. Johnson for help. Johnson, a strong supporter of civil rights, arranged for Longoria to be buried in Arlington National Cemetery with full military honors. Dr. Héctor García's family received insults and threats, but he never wavered. Dr. Cleo wholeheartedly supported her brother's work with the G. I. Forum and was a leader in the Auxiliary of the organization.

When farm workers in the Valley began to agitate for a higher minimum, she took an active interest in the struggle.

A strike began on June 1, 1966, when farm workers making eighty-five cents an hour at a melon-growing operation asked for their pay to be raised to a minimum wage of $1.25 an hour. Newspapers picked up the story of the low wages, unsanitary conditions, and poor medical care the workers received. Strikers and people sympathetic to their cause marched from Rio Grande City to Austin to demand better wages for the workers. Not content simply to lend her name to the movement, Dr. Cleo joined her brother Dr. Héctor García at the head of the strikers' march as it came through Corpus Christi.

Diplomatic, courteous, yet determined, she spoke out when there was a need. She was quick to join forces to improve conditions for the poor, who made up so many of her patients. She was active in efforts to improve the Corpus Christi school, strongly advocating for desegregation. She used her influence to support young activists, providing encouragement as well as financial help. Her focus on helping the underprivileged made her all the more venerated.

It took a stroke in 1994 to force Dr. Cleo to retire as a physician and limit her public involvement. She donated her books and many of her papers to Texas A&M University–Corpus Christi at that time, and her family donated the rest after her death on May 23, 2003. The papers are housed in the Special Collections & Archives Department of the Mary and Jeff Bell Library on the university campus, as are the papers of her brother Dr. Héctor García. The collections provide an invaluable research opportunity for those interested in the history of Hispanic America and Texas in particular as well as civil rights.

Dr. Cleo is buried in Seaside Memorial Park in Corpus Christi, but honors continued to come after her death. In 2006 the Tejano Genealogy Society of Austin created the Clotilde P. García Book Prize, awarding one thousand dollars annually to the best book that focuses on Texas's Hispanic heritage. In 2008 Corpus Christi renamed the city library Dr. Clotilde P. García Public Library.

Dr. Clotilde Pérez García's life impacted many people. She was a caring, personal physician to thousands of Hispanics in Corpus Christi over her forty-year career in medicine. She was an outstanding advocate for better health, better living conditions, and better wages for the poor. She advocated for desegregation. She was especially proud of her own heritage and prompted other Hispanics to feel the same pride. A lifelong scholar, she became a historian for South Texas. In honor of her long service to her community in medicine, education, and cultural heritage, she was one of the first twelve women inducted into the Texas Women's Hall of Fame in 1984.

DR. HÉCTOR PÉREZ GARCÍA (1914–1996)

Héctor and Clotilde García were just two of the over-
achievers among the seven children of José and Faustina
García. Six became physicians. Héctor was the second son,
three years older than Clotilde. Both were born in Mexico
and came to the United States as small children. Both followed their eldest brother, José Antonio García, to bachelor
degrees from the University of Texas and medical degrees
from the University of Texas Medical Branch in Galveston,
then to Corpus Christi to set up medical practice.

The sting of a teacher who said that no Mexican would
ever make an A in her class spurred him to a lifetime of
achievement. A school superintendent bragging about segregation led him into vigorous action involving civil rights on
behalf of Mexican Americans. After finishing medical school,
he served in the Medical Corps during World War II, rising
to the rank of major and earning the Bronze Star Medal.

He married Wanda Fusillo in Italy in 1945 and returned
to Corpus Christi where he cared for people without regard
for payment. Impatient with injustices against Mexican
Americans, he became a leader in the League of United Latin
American Citizens (LULAC). He fought for desegregation of
public schools. He marched with migrant workers seeking
higher wages and better working conditions. He opposed the
poll tax that penalized poor citizens who wanted to vote. He
was the first Mexican American to serve on the US Commission on Civil Rights.

He founded the American G. I. Forum to fight for educational and medical benefits for Mexican-American veterans. His involvement in the Felix Longoria incident focused national attention on discrimination against Mexican-American veterans. Through the Forum, he was active in support of the case in which the Supreme Court struck down a Texas law banning Mexican Americans from Texas grand juries.

Honors came from his service. The Dr. Héctor Peréz García Endowed Chair was created at Yale University. The main post office and a park in Corpus Christi are named for him. When writing her novel *Giant*, Edna Ferber consulted Héctor García and modeled the Mexican-American doctor in the book on his experiences.

Presidents Kennedy, Carter, and George H. W. Bush recognized his leadership in the area of civil rights. President Johnson appointed him an alternate ambassador to the United Nations. President Ronald Reagan awarded him the Presidential Medal of Freedom, the first Mexican American so honored. At his death, President Clinton praised him as "a national hero."[67]

Dr. Héctor García's papers and those of his sister Clotilde García are at Texas A&M University–Corpus Christi, where a nine-foot statue of him stands on campus.

MARIA GUADALUPE CAMPOS QUINTANILLA
(1937–   )
COURTESY OF GUADALUPE QUINTANILLA

María Guadalupe Campos Quintanilla

1937-[   ]

Love is a very powerful motivating factor, especially love for one's children. Couple that with ambition for those children to succeed, and the two become a force to be reckoned with. Lupe Quintanilla loved her children. She wanted the best for them, but they were struggling in school because of a language deficiency. Told that the children needed to speak English at home, the mother who spoke no English faced seemingly insurmountable obstacles trying to learn the language herself. No place would teach her English . . . until she made it happen by sheer determination. Her success spilled over to all three children. She shared her story to help others who were struggling in difficult situations. Her love for her children and her ambition for them became an ever-widening circle of influence to make the world better.

María Guadalupe Campos was born in Ojinaga, Chihuahua, Mexico, on October 25, 1937. She was a happy, healthy baby until her parents, Isabel and Angel Campos, divorced eighteen months later. When Isabel left, she took

Lupe with her. Shortly after that Lupe's sister Argelia was born.

Things turned bad quickly. Lupe became sick. She could not walk. Angel became concerned for his daughter. He took her to the doctor who told him Lupe should not return to her mother's care. Angel raced away with her to his parents' home in Nogales, Sonora. Under the care of her loving grandmother, Lupe quickly recovered.

Lupe's grandfather had a job inspecting boxcars that crossed the border into the United States, and Lupe often tagged along, amusing herself by picking up rocks and interesting things to put in her box of "treasures." Once, though, he was inspecting a carload of tomatoes. Lupe loved tomatoes. She helped herself to more and more until her stomach let her know that was not a good idea.

At the store her grandparents owned, Lupe learned to answer the phone and take orders, often surprising the person on the phone to hear a child's voice. The grandparents adored Lupe, indulged her with pets, and took many pictures, even one by a photographer of her sitting on a carnival horse in a cowboy outfit.

She entered school and quickly learned to read, but school came to an end when her grandparents moved to be near their oldest son. Her uncle had just finished medical school and was required to practice medicine in a tiny village in Guerro as payment for his free education. There was no school, but Lupe made up for it by teaching some younger boys and girls to read and do math.

When her uncle finished his term there, the family moved to Matamoros, Tamaulipas. She kept track of his patients and even learned to give shots by practicing on an orange. Now back in school, she was placed in the fourth grade and got to carry Mexico's flag in the school parade because she was the top student. Reading was her favorite subject. As an adult she still treasured her copies of *Pinocchio* and *A Thousand and One Nights*.

But school came to an end again after her grandmother lost the sight in one eye. They moved to an isolated farm where they raised cotton. They had lots of chickens and that attracted snakes. Lupe tried to get rid of them with her slingshot, but it didn't work. She asked for a gun, and her father, who was living in Brownsville, Texas, sent her his .22 caliber rifle. She became a crack shot and proved it years later when she made a better score at the shooting range than the Houston police chief.

Even without a school to attend, she spent hours reading stories by famous Spanish authors to her grandparents. She developed into a speed reader, her eyes reaching the bottom of the page before she had completed the first sentence. But even this came to an end when her grandmother lost her sight completely. The elderly couple moved into their son's house, but there was no room for Lupe. She went to live with her father and stepmother in the United States.

To enroll in school, she had to take an IQ test. Because it was in English, she couldn't answer the questions and made a very low score. The school placed her in the first grade where she could not understand what was being said. Since she was older, she was assigned to take the younger girls to the bathroom. She was embarrassed and unhappy. One day one of the men cutting grass spoke to her in Spanish, and she eagerly answered. The teacher overheard her and marched her to the principal's office. She had no idea why they were angry. She did not know that speaking Spanish was forbidden. But she did know that she would never go back there. Lupe Campos, age thirteen, dropped out of first grade.

Teachers today are more sensitive, and there are programs to help children of any culture learn English, but Lupe entered adulthood with no education credentials and no ability to speak English. She worked for a while as a housemaid. Then, at sixteen she married Cayetano Quintanilla. He had a good job as a dental technician, and she settled into married life. Victor was born in 1956, Mario in 1957, and Martha two years later. They had a nice house and took interesting vacations. Lupe was a good cook and learned to sew, making clever costumes for the children to wear in the Charro parade, part of a Brownsville festival celebrating cowboys.

The children however were not doing well at school. When Martha started to school, Lupe volunteered to help Spanish-speaking children. One day she noticed that the children were placed in different groups. The Red Birds spoke English, but the Yellow Birds where her child was spoke Spanish. Her sons had been in the Yellow Bird

group. The teacher told her that the boys were slow learners and had been placed in a group with others like them.
She didn't believe they were slow learners and questioned
the principal. He told her the children were handicapped
because they spoke only Spanish at home. They could not
function well in English. Remembering the humiliating
experience of her year in the first grade unable to understand English, she vowed it was not going to happen to
her children. She was not only going to be able to speak
English, she would learn spelling and grammar and everything else!

It was an easy thing to say, but much harder to do. She
first approached the person in charge of the volunteers
at the hospital where she delivered flowers and mail. She
asked to sit in the back of the class that trained aides, but
was told she needed a high school diploma. She went to
the high school and asked to sit in the back of the English
class. They told her that her school records listed her as
mentally retarded, the result of that IQ test. They would
not accept her.

She went back to the principal at her children's school.
Seeing how much she wanted to learn, he suggested that
the community college might have a course that would help
her. She rode the bus to Texas Southmost College on the
other side of town and went to the registrar's office only to
hear the clerk repeat that she could not enroll because she
had no high school certificate. Desperate, she left the office
and asked a passing student which car belonged to the

registrar. He pointed it out, and she sat down on the hood. When the registrar finally came out, she told him she was not moving until he let her in. He decided to give someone with this much determination a chance and granted her special permission to enroll. But, he warned, "If you don't make it, don't bother me anymore."[68]

Make it she did! Every semester she made the dean's list of top students. That did not mean everything came easy. She didn't know what algebra was, maybe some kind of spaghetti. The first session made her nauseous, but with the help of younger students, she passed.

Her family thought she would get tired and quit. As wife, mother, and student, she got up at 4:00 a.m. to study, took the long bus ride to school, returned at noon to prepare her husband's lunch, went back for afternoon classes, returning home in time to be there when her children got out of school. She completed her work at the community college and set her sights on a college degree from Pan American University (now University of Texas–Rio Grande Valley) in Edinburg, Texas. Two days a week she rode the sixty miles to Edinburg in a carpool. But she kept attending classes in Brownsville three days a week. She finished both schools at the same time, earning a bachelor of science degree *cum laude* (with honor) in 1969. Best of all, her children were thriving in school.

Lupe, hungry for more education, moved to Houston with her children. Her husband chose not to join them. She juggled coursework at the University of Houston, parent conferences, and attendance at her children's sports events. With finances tight, she graded exams and taught Spanish at the downtown YMCA to earn money. By 1971 she had earned a master's degree in Spanish and Latin-American literature, and the university quickly hired her, their first Mexican-American teacher. She earned the school's Teaching Excellence Award. She was put in charge of the Mexican-American Studies program, and soon headed the Bilingual Education program.

In 1976 she completed her doctor of education degree and became a university administrator, again the first Mexican American in that position at the University of Houston. This led fifteen years later to a position as assistant vice president for academic affairs. She counseled students, helped dropouts get enrolled again, handled funds for those needing financial aid, and checked to be sure students completed required courses for graduation.

A tragic event in Houston in 1977 made her aware that the language barrier worked both ways, sometimes with tragic consequences. The Houston police arrested a young Hispanic war veteran, and he died while in their custody. This led to riots. She knew the police needed to understand Hispanics and be able to talk to them. At the same time, Hispanics needed to understand what the police were saying. She realized there was a way to help both groups understand each other. She contacted the director of Ripley House, a community center in a heavily Spanish-speaking part of Houston.

Ripley House has played an important role in Houston's Hispanic community for nearly seventy years, providing recreation, education, medical, and legal services for thousands on a daily basis. There are programs and services for senior citizens as well as afterschool programs for children. Teens can learn career skills and get homework help. It was a busy place in 1977, and when a new building opened in 2001, more services became available. Today Ripley House has campuses in other locations to extend its services even further.

For Lupe Quintanilla, the building in the heart of a Hispanic community offered the perfect place to hold classes for police officers to learn Spanish. She and the director of Ripley House went to see Assistant Police Chief John Bales, and the three of them put a plan in place for officers to come to Ripley House twice a week to spend three hours listening, learning, and speaking street Spanish, the kind most likely spoken by the persons they were dealing with.

She spent time with officers finding out what words they needed to know. She read reports of accidents and family arguments. After making a list of all the words, she created little dictionaries small enough to fit in an officer's pocket. She developed a manual for officers to practice asking and answering questions. They learned to recognize important Spanish phrases for their own protection—such as "take away his gun" or "jump him from behind." She emphasized the need to be polite and especially never to say *Tú madre,* an insulting term to young Hispanic men. Instead they should use *mamá* for "mother."

But it was important for the officers to hear the words spoken. Rather than tape the programs so that officers heard only one type of voice, she arranged for a variety of speakers—men and women, both young and old, even children—to come and act as victims or suspects so that the officers would be familiar with the different sounds of spoken Spanish.

As participants talked at informal sessions, officers not only gained valuable understanding of what was being said, but they also came to understand cultural differences. Many were surprised to find that it made a difference how they asked for a name. The questions "What is your name?" and "What is your last name?" might not get the same answer. In Spanish, a person's surname is sometimes followed by the mother's maiden name. It was important for the officers to know the difference. The programs were a great success, and at the end of each course everyone enjoyed a fiesta with food and *folklórico* dances.

Lupe kept in contact with the police, especially to update the dictionaries as new names for drugs appeared on the street. And they called her to the station sometimes when they simply could not understand someone. Once, the person seemed to be speaking a strange form of Spanish and they could make no sense of it. She realized the person was speaking Portuguese, a language closely related to Spanish.

The success of the program led to requests for her to create similar manuals for other groups— firefighters, emergency personnel, airport police, drug enforcement officers, paramedics, and police dispatchers. Businesses also called on her to help employees who dealt with Spanish-speaking nations.

Because of her own school experience, she was particularly alarmed by the high dropout rate among Hispanic students. Working with actor Edward James Olmos, she helped create a television program called *Hispanic Dropouts: America's Time Bomb* that aired September 17, 1986. She was pleased to take part in the President's Advisory Commission on Educational Excellence for Hispanic Americans, because, she said, "I have more than textbook information about the issue. I have lived it."[69] She visited schools to encourage Hispanic students to stay in school, sharing her story of struggle and success. "The more you learn, the faster you get to the goal of what you want to be."[70]

As her story became known, *Reader's Digest* carried a story about her that was translated into thirty-seven languages. The July 1984 issue of *Ladies' Home Journal* named Guadalupe Quintanilla as the woman from Texas to receive its National Heroine Award. She was elected to both the National Hispanic Hall of Fame and the Hispanic Women's Hall of Fame. She received international attention when President Reagan appointed her alternate ambassador to the United Nations in 1984. Part of her speech before the assembly was in Spanish. The *Houston Post* chose her as one of Houston's Top Ten Leaders in 1986. She worked with Vice President George H. W. Bush to create laws that would be fair to everyone, and then after he became president he sent her to Vienna, Austria, in 1991 to address the World Conference on International Issues and Women's Affairs.

But her proudest accomplishment? That was her ability to brag, "When they call my house and ask for Dr. Quintanilla, we have to ask them 'Which one?' because there are four of us."[71] Victor Quintanilla and his sister Martha both earned law degrees, and Mario Quintanilla became a medical doctor.

Dr. Guadalupe Quintanilla made her own success and that of her children happen through her own efforts. She is modest about it. "I represent opportunity in this country."[72] She dismisses the hard times, refusing defeat. "If I'm not successful in something I want to do, I'm successful in finding out why I wasn't."[73]

She used as a guide for her life a verse from a poem by Amado Nervo that she translated as follows:

> *When I got to the end of my long journey through life,*
> *I discovered that I have always been the architect of my own destiny.*
> *If I planted roses along the way, I harvested roses.*
> *And I need not look at the thorns, but look at the roses.*[74]

WORDS FOR BETTER UNDERSTANDING

Training sessions conducted for Houston police officers provided them with valuable knowledge about how to deal with Spanish-speaking individuals. Since it was unlikely that these individuals would be speaking Castilian Spanish, the officers needed to know common street Spanish. For example, in Spanish *cuete* usually means "firecracker," but in street Spanish it means "gun." *Fila* means "edge," but on the streets it means "knife." *Camión* is the word for "truck," but the word in street Spanish is *troca*.

The officers also learned words and phrases not to say. "Drop it" is the normal English used to tell someone to drop a gun, but the Spanish word *tírelo* can also mean "throw it." Instead, officers learned to say *suéltelo*. That means "let go of it." After one officer learned to use that term, he confronted a suspect and yelled *"Suéltelo!"* The sound of a white officer speaking Spanish so startled the suspect that he dropped his gun.

Another officer almost had a death on his hands when he responded to a robbery in progress call. He approached a man holding a gun and kept saying, "Drop it! Drop it!" The man slowly raised the gun and emptied the bullets out on the floor. The waitress ran in to say the robbers were gone. The officer had almost shot the cook.

Teenagers who came to help the officers speak and understand Spanish once played a trick on them. They got a big laugh at the officers' reaction after they wrote *"El burro sabe más que tú." (the donkey knows more than you) on the board. This is a familiar Spanish sentence that helps children remember vowels. The officers laughed too when they understood the joke.

Engaging in the training sessions not only helped the officers understand Spanish, it helped both officers and community to be more comfortable with each other. One direct outcome of efforts to improve relations between the groups was the hiring of Hispanic officers. And in 2016, Art Acevedo became the first Hispanic chief of police in Houston, Texas.

Notes

1 Pike, *An Account of Expedition.*

2 Harris, "The Reminiscences of Mrs. Dilue Harris," 92.

3 Ibid., 161.

4 Ibid., 69.

5 Ibid., 215.

6 Michael L. Tate, "Parker, Quanah (ca. 1852-1911)." Encyclopedia of the Great Plains. http://plainshumanities.unl.edu/encyclopoedia/doc/egp.na .p081. Accessed June 3, 2017.

7 William T. Hagan, *Quanah Parker, Comanche Chief* (Norman: University of Oklahoma, 1995), 57, as quoted in Frankel, *The Searchers.*

8 Robertson and Robertson, *Panhandle Pilgrimage*, 151.

9 Goodnight, Mary Ann, in Robertson, p.151.

10 Shelton, "Lizzie E. Johnson: A Cattle Queen of Texas," 361.

11 Ibid., 362.

12 Ibid., 364.

13 Burks, "A Woman Trail Driver," 305.

14 Ken Grissom, "Adair's Day: Activist Honored at Park Dedication," *Houston Post*, October 23, 1977, as quoted in Black, "Female Community Leaders in Houston, Texas," 229.

15 Karkabi, " 'Fire in Her Belly,' " quoting El Franco Lee.

16 Christia Adair, "Interview with Christia Adair: Black Women Oral History Project," Cambridge, MA: Schlesinger Library, Radcliffe College, 1978, as quoted in Black, "Female Community Leaders in Houston, Texas," 162.

17 "Interview with Christia Adair," April 25, 1977, Radcliffe College, *in The Black Women Oral History Project,* Vol. 1, 58–59, as quoted in Winegarten, *Black Texas Women: A Sourcebook,* Document 127: Mothers Club.

18 Adair, "Interview," as quoted in Black, "Female Community Leaders in Houston, Texas," 223.

19 Winegarten, *Black Texas Women: A Sourcebook,* Document 232: Christia Adair Becomes a Democrat.

20 Ibid., Document 169.

21 Ellen Bernstein, "Long Road to Freedom," *Corpus Christi Caller-Times,* February 21, 1999, statement by Harold Dunton, as quoted in Black, "Female Community Leaders in Houston, Texas," 188.

22 Willie L. Gay, "Interview by Linda Black," tape recording, November 30, 2007, Houston, Texas, quoting Christa Adair, as quoted in Black, "Female Community Leaders in Houston, Texas," 174.

Notes

23 Coutinho, "Survivor, 104, Recalls Night of 1900 Storm."

24 Pugh, "THE BIG ONE."

25 Moran, "ECHOES OF THE STORM."

26 Coutinho, "Survivor, 104, Recalls Night of 1900 Storm."

27 Stillwell, *I'll Gather My Geese, 10.*

28 Ibid., 10.

29 Ibid., 38.

30 Ibid,, 65.

31 Kiepper, "Earning Her Spurs."

32 Brian M. Simmons, "From Belgium to 'Rough-and-Tumble Waco': The Academy of the Sacred Heart and the Sisters of St. Mary of Namur." Quoted from May 24, 1946, article in The Waco Tribune. http://blogs.baylor.edu/texascollection/2016/05/10/from-belgium-to-rough-and-tumble-waco-the-academy-of-the-sacred-heart-and-the-sisters-of-st-mary-of-namur/. Accessed July 25, 2017.

33 McKanna, Interview with Jean Everett.

34 Ibid.

35 Amelia Earhart, note to George Putnam, 1937.

36 Adele, *Spirited Journey,* 81.

37 Ibid.

38 Ibid., 82.

39 Winegarten, *Black Texas Women: 150 Years of Trial and Triumph,* 148.

40 Adele, *Spirited Journey,* 82.

41 Ibid., 83.

42 Curlee, "Gunter, Alma Pennell."

43 Hunt, *I Am Annie Mae,* 5.

44 Ibid., 67.

45 Ibid.

46 Ibid., 85.

47 Ibid.

48 Ibid., 61.

49 Ibid., 121.

50 Cayleff, BABE, 37.

51 Babe Didrikson Zaharias, *The Life I've Led* (New York: Dell Publishing Company, 1976), 27, as quoted in Cayleff, BABE, 46.

52 Col. M. J. McCombs, quoted in "Looking 'em Over," *Dallas Dispatch,* n.d., as quoted in Cayleff, BABE, 49.

53 William Oscar John and Nancy Williamson, *"Whatta-Gal" The Babe Didrikson Story* (Boston: Little, Brown, 1975), as quoted in Cayleff, BABE, 73.

54 Bob Hope, as quoted in Cayleff, BABE, 147.

55 www.pbs.org/ladybird/earlyyears/earlyyears_index.html.

Notes

56 Gillette, *Lady Bird Johnson*, 15.

57 Ibid,, 14.

58 Ibid., 20.

59 Russell, *Lady Bird*, 35.

60 Gillette, *Lady Bird Johnson*, 27.

61 Claudia T. Johnson, *Lady Bird Johnson*, vii.

62 Ibid., 556.

63 Ibid., 782.

64 Kreneck, "Dr. Clotilde P. Garcia."

65 Garcia, Clotilde P., "Escandón, José de."

66 Kreneck, "Dr. Clotilde P. Garcia."

67 "Hector P. Garcia: A Texas Legend."

68 Registrar, Texas Southmost College, as quoted by Guadalupe Quintanilla in Barbara Karkabi, I Have Lived It," Houston Chronicle, January 14, 1992, 4D.

69 Barbara Karkabi, "I Have Lived It," Houston Chronicle, January 14, 1992, 1D.

70 Guadalupe Quintanilla, quoted in Veronica Flores, "Love for Children Drives Brownsville Native," *Brownsville Herald,* October 18, 1988.

71 Quintanilla, quoted in Juan Espinosa, "Hard Experiences Lead to Helping People Understand," *Pueblo Chieftain*, April 10, 1993.

72 Molly Ancelin, "Architect of Her Own Destiny: Guadalupe Quintanilla," *Houston Digest*, June 25, 1984, 18.

73 Ibid.

74 Author interview with Guadalupe Quintanilla, April 19, 1994.

Bibliography

María Gertrudis Pérez Cordero Cassiano 1790–1832

Acosta, Teresa Paloma. "Cassiano, María Gertrudis Pérez." *Handbook of Texas Online*. https://tshaonline.org/handbook/online/articles/fcadh, accessed August 2, 2017.

Beeman, Cynthia J. "Maria Betancourt." *Women in Texas History: A Project of the Ruthe Winegarten Memorial Foundation for Texas Women's History*. www.womenintexashistory.org/audio/cassiano/, accessed August 4, 2017.

"Canary Islanders Who Came to Texas, Arriving in San Antonio on March 9, 1731." https://www.familytreedna.com/public/canarians -of-texas/, accessed August 3, 2017.

De La Teja, Jesús. "San Fernando de Béxar." *Handbook of Texas Online*. https://tshaonline.org/handbook/online/articles/hvs16, accessed August 2, 2017.

Gaines, Ann Graham. "San Fernando Cathedral." *Handbook of Texas Online*. https://tshaonline.org/handbook/online/articles/ivs01, accessed August 3, 2017.

García, Clotilde P. "Hinojosa de Ballí, Rosa María." *Handbook of Texas Online*. https://tshaonline.org/handbook/online/articles/fhi50, accessed August 4, 2017.

Gibson, Steve. "Béxar Genealogy." http://bexargenealogy.com/, accessed August 2–5, 2017.

Holmes, Jack D. "Cordero y Bustamante, Manuel Antonio." *Handbook of Texas Online*. https://tshaonline.org/handbook/online/articles/fco68, accessed August 2, 2017.

Jackson, Jack. "Álvarez Travieso, Vicente." *Handbook of Texas Online*. https://www.tshaonline.org/handbook/online/articles/fal77, accessed August 4, 2017.

Bibliography

Murr, Erika. "San Antonio de Bexar Presidio." In *Handbook of Texas
    Online*. https://tshaonline.org/handbook/online/articles/uqs02,
    accessed August 2, 2017.

Parker, Edith Olbrich. "Maria Gertrudis Perez Cordero Cassiano
    (1790–1832)." In Evelyn M. Carrington, ed. *Women in Early Texas*.
    Austin: Texas State Historical Association, 1994, reprint. Origi-
    nally published by American Association of University Women,
    1975. [*Note*: This is a deeply flawed account with numerous
    mistakes.]

Pike, Zebulon Montgomery. *An Account of Expedition to the Sources of the
    Mississippi and through the Western Parts of Louisiana*. Philadelphia:
    Conrad, 1918, as quoted in Jack D. L. Holmes, "Cordero y Busta-
    mante, Manuel Antonio." https://tshaonline.org/handbook/online/
    articles/fco68, accessed August 4, 2017.

Strong, Bernice. "José, Cassiano." *Handbook of Texas Online*. https://
    tshaonline.org/handbook/online/articles/fcaan, accessed August 2,
    2017.

Tarin, Randell G. "Second Flying Company of San Carlos de Parras."
    Handbook of Texas Online. https://tshaonline.org/handbook/online/
    articles/qhs01, accessed August 3, 2017.

Winegarten, Ruthe. *Texas Women: A Pictorial History From Indians to
    Astronauts*. Austin: Eakin Press, n.d., 12.

Dilue Rose Harris 1825–1914

Crawford, Ann Fears and Crystal Sasse Ragsdale. "Texas Girl." *Women
    in Texas: Their Lives, Their Experiences, Their Accomplishments*.
    Austin: Eakin Press, 1982, 38–49.

Exley, Jo Ella Powell. "Dilue Rose Harris." *Texas Tears and Texas
    Sunshine: Voices of Frontier Women*. College Station: Texas A&M
    University Press, 1985, 53–74.

Flachmeier, Jeanette Hastedt. "Dilue Rose Harris (1825–1914)." In
    Evelyn M. Carrington, ed. *Women in Early Texas*, 2nd ed. Austin:
    Texas State Historical Association, 1994, 101–7.

Bibliography

Harris, Dilue Rose. "The Reminiscences of Mrs. Dilue Harris." In 3 parts. *Quarterly of the Texas State Historical Association* IV (1900): 85–127; 155–89; VII (1904): 214–22.

Lang, Herbert H. "Harris, Dilue Rose." *The New Handbook of Texas in Six Volumes.* Austin: Texas State Historical Association, 1996, Vol. 3, 473.

Cynthia Ann Parker 1826–1871

Carlson, Paul H. and Tom Crum. *Myth, Memory and Massacre: The Pease River Capture of Cynthia Ann Parker.* Lubbock: Texas Tech University Press, 2010.

"Fort Parker Massacre." https://en.wikipedia.org/wiki/Fort_Parker_massacre, accessed June 22, 2017.

Frankel, Glenn. *The Searchers: The Making of an American Legend.* New York: Bloomsbury, 2013.

Friend, Llerena B. "Parker, John." *The New Handbook of Texas in Six Volumes.* Austin: Texas State Historical Association, 1996, Vol. 5, 60.

Hacker, Margaret Schmidt. "Parker, Cynthia Ann." *The New Handbook of Texas in Six Volumes.* Austin: Texas State Historical Association, 1996, Vol. 5, 57–58.

Hesler, Samuel B. "Pilgrim Primitive Baptist Church." *The New Handbook of Texas in Six Volumes.* Austin: Texas State Historical Association, 1996, Vol. 5, 205.

Hosmer, Brian C. "Parker, Quanah." *The New Handbook of Texas in Six Volumes.* Austin: Texas State Historical Association, 1996, Vol. 5, 61–62.

Lipscomb, Carol A. "Comanche Indians." *The New Handbook of Texas in Six Volumes.* Austin: Texas State Historical Association, 1996, Vol. 2, 242–45.

Plummer, Rachel. https://en.wikipedia.org/wiki/Rachel_Plummer, accessed June 22, 2017.

Selden, Jr., Jack K. "Parker, James W." *The New Handbook of Texas in Six Volumes.* Austin: Texas State Historical Association, 1996, Vol. 5, 59–60.

Bibliography

_____. "Parker, Silas M." *The New Handbook of Texas in Six Volumes.* Austin: Texas State Historical Association, 1996, Vol. 5, 62–63.

"Texas State Archives—Land Grant Database." www.rootsweb.ancestry .com/~txlimest/landrecords/parker-landgrant.htm, accessed June 23, 2017.

Wellman, Paul I. "Cynthia Ann Parker." *Chronicles of Oklahoma.* Oklahoma City: Oklahoma Historical Society, Vol. 12, No. 2, 1934. http://digital.library.okstate.edu/Chronicles/v012/v012p163.html, accessed June 21, 2017.

Mary Ann "Molly" Dyer Goodnight 1839–1926

Anderson, Greta. *Remarkable Texas Women.* Guilford, CT: Morris Book Publishing, 1973.

Crawford, Ann Fears, and Crystal Sasse Ragsdale. *Women in Texas: Their Lives, Their Experiences, Their Accomplishments.* Austin: Eakin Press, 1982.

Hagan, William T. *Charles Goodnight, Father of the Texas Panhandle.* Norman: University of Oklahoma Press, 2007.

Haley, J. Evetts. *Charles Goodnight: Cowman and Plainsman.* Norman: University of Oklahoma Press, 1936.

Hutchison, Kay Bailey. *Unflinching Courage: Pioneering Women Who Shaped Texas.* New York: HarperCollins, 2013.

Roach, Joyce Gibson. "Goodnight, Mary Ann Dyer." *The New Handbook of Texas in Six Volumes.* Austin: Texas State Historical Association, 1996, Vol. 3, 243–44.

Robertson, Pauline Durrett, and R. L. Robertson, *Panhandle Pilgrimage.* Amarillo, TX: Paramount Publishing Company, 1978.

Elizabeth Ellen "Lizzie" Johnson Williams 1843–1924

Burks, Amanda. "A Woman Trail Driver." J. Marvin Hunter, ed. *The Trail Drivers of Texas,* 2nd ed. New York: Argosy-Antiquarian Ltd., 1963, Vol. 1, 295–305 (first published 1920–1923).

Bibliography

"The Cattle Queen of Texas—Elizabeth Johnson Williams." http:// sweetheartsofthewest.blogspot.com/2016/07/the-cattle-queen-of -texas-elizabeth.html, accessed June 14, 2017.

Connolly, Jeff. "Hit the Trail in High Places." J. Marvin Hunter, ed. *The Trail Drivers of Texas*, 2nd ed. New York: Argosy-Antiquarian Ltd., 1963, Vol. 1, 187–93 (first published 1920–1923).

Crawford, Ann Fears, and Crystal Sasse Ragsdale. *Women in Texas: Their Lives, Their Experiences, Their Accomplishments.* Austin: Eakin Press, 1982, 122–34.

Duncan, Roberta S. "Williams, Elizabeth Ellen Johnson." *The New Handbook of Texas in Six Volumes.* Austin: Texas State Historical Association, 1996, Vol. 6, 980–81.

Elizabeth Ellen "Lizzie" Johnson Williams. https://www.findagrave .com/cgi-bin/fg.cgi?page=gr&GRid=24347168, accessed June 14, 2017.

Hutchison, Kay Bailey. "Lizzie Johnson Williams." *Unflinching Courage: Pioneering Women Who Shaped Texas.* New York: HarperCollins, 2013, 260–65.

"Lizzie Johnson Williams—the Cattle Queen of Texas." Texas General Land Office Save Texas History Program, May 5, 2016. https:// medium.com/save-texas-history/lizzie-johnson-williams-the-cattle -queen-of-texas-9660c82cd994, accessed June 14, 2017.

Sawyer, Bobbie Jean. "Lizzie Johnson Williams, the Texas Cattle Queen Who Made History." *Wide Open Country*, www.wideopencountry .com/lizzie-johnson-williams/, accessed June 14, 2017.

Shelton, Emily Jones. "Lizzie E. Johnson: A Cattle Queen of Texas." *Southwestern Historical Quarterly*, Vol. 50, no. 3, January 1947, 349–66.

Christia V. Daniels Adair 1893–1989

Black, Linda L. "Female Community Leaders in Houston, Texas: A Study of the Education of Ima Hogg and Christia Daniels Adair." PhD diss., Texas A&M University, 2008.

Bibliography

Duggar, Ronnie. "Randolph, Frankie Carter." *The New Handbook of Texas in Six Volumes*. Austin: Texas State Historical Association, 1996, Vol. 5, 439–40.

Jones, Nancy Baker. "Adair, Christia V. Daniels." *The New Handbook of Texas in Six Volumes*. Austin: Texas State Historical Association, 1996, Vol. 1, 21–22.

Karkabi, Barbara. "'Fire in Her Belly': Hundreds Honor Lifelong Civil-Rights Fight." *Houston Chronicle*, January 8, 1990.

Winegarten, Ruthe. *Black Texas Women: A Sourcebook: Documents, Biographies, Timeline*. Austin: University of Texas Press, 1996.

———. *Black Texas Women: 150 Years of Trial and Triumph*. Austin: University of Texas Press, 1995.

Lorraine Rey Isaacs Hofeller 1896–2002

Abram, Lynwood. "Hofeller, 106, Survivor of the 1900 Galveston Hurricane." *Houston Chronicle*, July 20, 2002.

Cartwright, Gary. *Galveston: A History of the Island*. Fort Worth: TCU Press, 1991.

Cline, Isaac M. "Special Report on the Galveston Hurricane of September 8, 1900." www.history.noaa.gov/stories_tales/cline2 .html, accessed June 7, 2017.

Coutinho, Juliana. "Survivor, 104, Recalls Night of 1900 Storm." *Galveston County Daily News*, September 9, 2000.

"Galveston's Response to the Hurricane of 1900." http://texasalmanac .com/topics/history/galvestons-response-hurricane-1900, accessed June 12, 2017.

Hofeller, Lorraine Isaacs. Interview, https://www.beth-israel.org, accessed June 7, 2017.

Jenevieve1350. "1900 Galveston Hurricane—The Survivor's Stories— The Orphanage." https://www.wattpad.com/1431481-1900 -galveston-hurricane-the-survivor%27s-stories, accessed January 30, 2017.

Bibliography

"Last Galveston Storm Survivor Dies at 106." *Texas City Sun,* July 21, 2002.

"Last Survivor of Great Storm. . . ." *Texas City Sun,* July 21, 2002.

McComb, David G. *Galveston.* Austin: Texas State Historical Association, 2000.

Moran, Kevin. "ECHOES OF THE STORM/104-Year-Old Tells How She Survived 1900 Hurricane." *Houston Chronicle,* September 7, 2000.

Pugh, Clifford. "THE BIG ONE/ Most Gulf Coast Residents Have Heard About the Killer Hurricane of 1900, But Lorraine Isaacs Hofeller Remembers It." *Houston Chronicle,* September 11, 1995.

"The Sisters of Charity Orphanage." The 1900 Storm: Remembering the Great Hurricane, September 8, 1900. www.1900storm.com/ orphanage.html, accessed June 11, 2017.

"Why Do Hurricanes Hit the East Coast of the U.S. but Never the West Coast." https://www.scientificamerican.com/article/why -do-hurricanes-hit-the-east-coast-of-the-u-s-but-never-the-west -coast/, accessed June 7, 2017.

Hallie Crawford Stillwell 1897–1997

"Hallie Stillwell: 1994 Inductee Business and Professional Leader- ship (1897–1997)." www.twu.edu/twhf/honorees/hallie-stillwell/, accessed July 17, 2017.

Kelley, Lynn. "Stillwell, Hallie Crawford." https://tshaonline.org/ handbook/online/articles/fstve, accessed July 17, 2017.

Kiepper, E. Dan. "Earning Her Spurs." http://tpwmagazine.com/ archive/2011/may/legend/, accessed August 1, 2017.

"Pancho Villa." http://www.historyh.com/topics/pancho-villa, accessed July 17, 2017.

"Pancho Villa: Military Leader (1878–1923)." https://www.biography .com/people/pancho-villa-9518733, accessed July 17, 2017.

Bibliography

Stillwell, Hallie Crawford. *I'll Gather My Geese.* College Station, TX: Texas A&M Press, 1991.

Thomas, Robert McG., Jr. "Hallie C. Stillwell, a Rancher and Texas Legend, Dies at 99." www.nytimes.com/1997/08/24/us/hallie-c-stillwell-a-rancher-and-Texas-legend-dies-at-99.html, accessed July 17, 2017.

Thorpe, Helen. "Hallie and Farewell." www.texasmonthly.com/the -culture/hallie-and-farewell/, accessed July 17, 2017.

Donna Edith Whatley McKanna 1899–1986

Anderson, H. Allen. "McKanna, Edith Whatley." https://tshaonline .org/handbook/online/articles/fmcdd, accessed July 8, 2017.

McKanna, Edith. Interview with Jean Everett, Snyder, Texas, as quoted in "Scurrily Speaking," Scurry County Historical Survey Committee newsletter, November 1971, mimeograph.

"National Ranching Heritage Center." www.depts.ttu.edu/nrhc/, accessed July 20, 2017.

Parks, Aline. *Snyder Scrapbook: From Hidetown to Boom Town.* Snyder, TX: Privately printed, 1998, 55–57.

Rickman, Sarah Byrn. "National WASP WWII Museum: Avenger Field Sweetwater, Texas." http://waspmuseum.org/, accessed July 22, 2017.

Scurry County Museum. *Snyder and Scurry County. Images of America.* Charleston, SC: Arcadia Publishing, 2012, 77, 85.

Wackerfuss, Andrew T. "Women's Airforce Service Pilots (WASP)." www.afhistory.af.mil/FAQs/Fact-Sheets/Article/458964/ womens-airforce-service-pilots-wasp/, accessed July 22, 2017.

"Women's Airforce Service Pilots (WASP)." www.twu.edu/library/wasp .asp, accessed July 22, 2017.

Alma Pennell Gunter 1909–1983

Adele, Lynne. *Spirited Journey: Self-Taught Texas Artists of the Twentieth Century.* The University of Texas at Austin, exhibition organized by the Archer M. Huntington Art Gallery, 1947.

Bibliography

Curlee, Randall. "Gunter, Alma Pennell." *The New Handbook of Texas in Six Volumes*. Austin: Texas State Historical Association, 1996, Vol. 3, 387–88.

Winegarten, Ruthe. *Black Texas Women: 150 Years of Trial and Triumph*. Austin: University of Texas Press, 1995.

Annie Mae McDade Prosper Hunt 1909–2003

"Annie Mae Hunt." Women in Texas History, www.womenintexas history.org/audio/annie-mae-hunt/, accessed May 20, 2017.

Hunt, Annie Mae. *I Am Annie Mae*, Ruthe Winegarten, ed. Austin: Rosegarden Press, 1983.

Winegarten, Ruthe. *Texas Women, a Pictorial History from Indians to Astronauts*. Austin: Eakin Press, n.d.

Mildred Ella "Babe" Didrikson Zaharias 1911–1956

Cayleff, Susan E. *BABE: The Life and Legend of Babe Didrikson Zaharias*. Urbana: University of Illinois Press, 1995.

_____. "Zaharias, Mildred Ella Didrikson." *The New Handbook of Texas in Six Volumes*. Austin: Texas State Historical Association, 1996, Vol. 6, 1138–39.

"A History of Girls Playing Tackle Football." www.angelfire.com/sports/womenfootball/princesses/timeline.html, accessed June 28, 2017.

"Mildred Didrikson." https://www.olympic.org/mildred-didrikson, accessed June 29, 2017.

Schwartz, Larry. "The Terrific Tomboy." https://espn.go.com/sports century/features/00194636.html, accessed June 30, 2017.

Wakeman, Nancy. *Babe Didrikson Zaharias: Driven to Win*. Minneapolis: Lerner Publications Company, 2000.

Claudia Alta "Lady Bird" Taylor Johnson 1912–2007

Anthony, Carl. "Who Is a First Lady?" http://www.firstladies.org/blog/who-is-a-first-lady/, accessed July 5, 2017.

Bibliography

Caroli, Betty Boyd. *Lady Bird and Lyndon: The Hidden Story of a Marriage That Made a President.* New York: Simon & Schuster Paperbacks, 2015.

"Claudia Taylor (Lady Bird) Johnson." https://www.whitehouse.gov/1600/first-ladies/ladybirdjohnson, accessed May 29, 2017.

Crawford, Ann Fears, and Crystal Sasse Ragsdale. *Women in Texas: Their Lives, Their Experiences, Their Accomplishments.* Austin: Eakin Press, 1982.

"First Lady Biography: Lady Bird Johnson." www.firstladies.org/biographies/firstladies.aspx?biography=37, accessed May 25, 2017.

Gillette, Michael L. *Lady Bird Johnson: An Oral History.* New York: Oxford University Press, 2012.

Johnson, Claudia T. *Lady Bird Johnson: A White House Diary.* New York: Holt, Rinehart and Winston, 1970.

"Lady Bird Johnson." www.lbjlibrary.org/lyndon-baines-johnson/lady-bird-johnson/, accessed May 27, 2017.

"Lady Bird Johnson." www.pbs.org/ladybird/earlyyears/earlyyears_index.html, accessed June 4, 2017.

"Lyndon Baines Johnson." www.lbjlibrary.org/lyndon-baines-johnson/lbj-biography/, accessed June 4, 2017.

Russell, Jan Jarboe. *Lady Bird: A Biography of Mrs. Johnson.* New York: Scribner, 1999.

Clotilde Pérez García 1917–2003

Abigail, R. Matt, and Hugo Martinez. "García, Clotilde Pérez." www.tshaonline.org/handbook/online/articles/fgaay, accessed July 23, 2017.

"Dr. Clotilde P. García Papers." https://www.utmb.edu/drgarcia/early.htm, accessed July 23, 2017.

Garcia, Clotilde P. "Escandón, José de." https://tshaonline.org/handbook/online/articles/fes01, accessed July 23, 2017.

"Hector P. Garcia: A Texas Legend." https://www.utmb.edu/drgarcia/, accessed July 29, 2017.

Bibliography

Kreneck, Thomas H. "Dr. Clotilde P. Garcia: Physician, Activist, and First Lady of Hispanic Genealogy." https://rattler.tamucc.edu/dept/special/garciacleobio.html, accessed January 22, 2017.

Rozeff, Norman. "García, Hector Pérez." https://tshaonline.org/handbook/online/articles/fga52, accessed July 29, 2017.

María Guadalupe Campos Quintanilla 1937–

In 1994 I interviewed Guadalupe Quintanilla in her office on the University of Houston campus and by telephone on March 24, 26, 27, 31 and April 11 and 19 for my book *Guadalupe Quintanilla: Leader of the Hispanic Community* (Berkeley Heights, NJ: Enslow Publishers, 1995).

I attended a Cross Cultural Communication Program training session, April 19, 1994.

Ancelin, Molly, "Architect of Her Own Destiny: Guadalupe Quintanilla," *Houston Digest*, June 25, 1984, 18.

Author interviews with Guadalupe Quintanilla, March 24, 26, 27, and 31, 1994

Author interviews with Guadalupe Quintanilla, April 11 and 19, 1994.

Espinosa, Juan, "Hard Experiences Lead to Helping People Understand," *Pueblo Chieftain*, April 10, 1993.

Flores, Veronica, "Love for Children Drives Brownsville Native," *Brownsville Herald*, October 18, 1988.

Karkabi, Barbara, "I Have Lived It," *Houston Chronicle*, January 14, 1992.

Wade, Mary Dodson, *Guadalupe Quintanilla: Leader of the Hispanic Community* (Berkeley Heights, NJ: Enslow Publishers, 1995.

Index

Index

Index

197–98, 200, 201; papers of,
208–209; Royal American
Order of Isabella the Catholic,
206; siblings, 202, 206; son,
202–203; social service, 205,
206, 208; teacher, 205–206;
Texas Women's Hall of Fame,
206. *See also* García, Héctor.
García, Héctor, 206, 208, 210–11,
See also American G.I. Forum;
Giant (movie); Longoria, Felix.
Giant (movie), 211
Golden Cyclones, 170
Goodnight, Charles, 41, 45, 52,
53–53, 57, 58, 59, 60. *See also*
Hubbard, Cleo.
Goodnight College, 59
Goodnight, Mary Ann Dyer
(Molly): appreciation of, 57;
brothers, 52, 55, 57; childhood,
49; marriage, 55; parents, 49;
"Mother of the Buffalo", 49;
"Mother of the Panhandle",
59; Pueblo, Colorado, life in,
54–55; teacher, 52, 54.
Goodnight, Texas, 58–59
Goodnight-Loving Trail, 53–54
Governor's Palace, San Antonio
1, 5–6, 8
Granada, María Robíana Bethén-
court, 4, 11
Gunter, Alma Pennell: art, love
of, 136, 138–39, 140; art as

therapy, 140; art competitions,
139, 141; art exhibitions, 144;
childhood, 135; education:
high school, 136; college,
136–138; family, 135, 136;
marriage, 140; occupations:
menial jobs, 136; nursing,
139–40; paintings, ideas for,
142–43; statement paintings,
143–44. *See Also* Segregation.
Gunter paintings: *Animals' Ark*,
144; *Dinner on the Grounds*,
143; *Pretty Mama, 143; Saturday Afternoon*, 142; *The Haves
and the Have-nots*, 143; *Winter
Cry,* 143

Harding, Warren G., 85–86
Harris County Democrats, 91
Harris, Dilue Rose: childhood,
15–16, 19, children, 26; chores,
19, 22; education, 20–21, 24;
entertainment, 19, 21; marriage, 25–26; parents: father,
15, 16, 18, 20, 21, 22, 23, 24,
25; mother 15, 18, 20, 21, 22,
23, 24; "The Reminiscences of
Mrs. Dilue Harris", 26; siblings 15–16, 18, 19, 20, 22, 24
Harrisburg, 18, 23, 24
Hispanic heritage, 205–206
Hofeller, Lorraine Rey Isaacs:
brother, 96, 99, 104; childhood,

Index

Index

Index

Index

Index

About the Author

Author **Mary Dodson Wade** lives in Houston, Texas. She spent twenty-five years as an elementary librarian and has published more than fifty books. She maintains membership in the Texas State Historical Association, Western Writers of America, Women Writing the West, the Texas Council for the Social Studies, Society of Children's Book Writers and Illustrators, and the Texas Library Association.